FROM
AUDIENCE
TO
ZEAL

FROM
AUDIENCE
TO
ZEAL

The ABCs of Finding, Crafting, and Telling a Great Story

A selection of tips, tricks, and meditations
on the art and craft of effective storytelling

LAURA S. PACKER

storyteller, writer, real-time dreamer

The Small-Tooth-Dog Publishing Group
Tolleson, Arizona USA

From Audience to Zeal: The ABCs of Finding, Crafting, and Telling a Great Story
Written by Laura S. Packer

Published 2019
The Small-Tooth-Dog Publishing Group
P.O. Box 392
Tolleson, Arizona 85353 USA
communication@smalltoothdog.com

ISBN: 9781947408036
Library of Congress Control Number: 2018946666

Typeset by Medlar Publishing Solutions Pvt Ltd., India

This book is dedicated to the memories of
Brother Blue, Harvey Packer, and Kevin Brooks.

Table of contents

About this book

Welcome to *From Audience to Zeal: The ABCs of Finding, Crafting, and Telling a Great Story*. This project grew out of the A–Z blog challenge, an annual event where bloggers post a daily alphabet on any given topic. Since I am a storyteller, it seemed fitting that I write about storytelling.

I loved this challenge. I've always enjoyed thinking about and analyzing the arts I practice, so this gave me a structured way to discuss and codify it. You can read the original posts and many other thoughts about storytelling on my blog, truestorieshonestlies.blogspot.com. This book contains many of the original posts and about 50% more new material, so even if you've followed my blog, there is new stuff here you may find instructive and inspiring.

I hope you find this book useful. It is by no means comprehensive; I cover a lot of topics and don't delve deeply into most, while there are others I didn't touch upon at all. I intend to answer questions and send you on the journey to learn more. While you can read this book from cover-to-cover if you choose, it is written as a reference book with mentions of other entries you may find useful, where appropriate. If you want to dig deeper, contact me and we can arrange coaching or workshops in your area. If you'd like to receive more storytelling information, please sign up for my mailing list at laurapacker.com. I will never spam you or share your email address. What's more, as an exclusive offer for readers of this book, you can receive occasional updates, exercises, and sneak peeks into new storytelling thoughts by emailing with the title *ABC updates* to laura@laurapacker. com. If you have suggestions for new topics, I would love to hear them.

The *Audience to Zeal* workbook, also published by Small-Tooth-Dog Publishing Group, complements this book. The companion workbook includes ideas and exercises for many topics and specific applications, such as teaching young children or strategic planning. It also includes additional resources should you wish to dig deeper into a topic.

Your story matters. We must hear each other to understand the world and we must be heard to know we are part of a community. If there is anything I can do to help you on your storytelling journey, please contact me.

I hope you find your happily ever after and that it brings you joy, adventure, and light.

With best wishes,
Laura

P.S. Okay, I know, it doesn't start with Audience. Think of that as a little extra treat.

About Laura Packer

Laura Packer knows that the best way to the truth is through a good story. For almost three decades, Laura has told, taught, ranted, raved, consulted, and considered storytelling around the world. Whether folktale or true, epic or flash, her stories captivate and amuse audiences in venues as varied as schools and theaters, assisted living facilities and arts festivals, private events and on the streets. Among other accolades, she is the winner of the 2010 National Storytelling Network Oracle Award; the 2012 League for the Advancement of New England Storytelling Brother Blue Award; 2016 and 2018 Best in KC Fringe; 2018 Minnesota Grand Slam Champion; three-time semi-finalist in the Boston Big Mouth Off Slam Competition; and was a finalist in the Philadelphia Best Slammers in the World Competition.

Laura is the sole proprietor of thinkstory llc, one of the foremost organizational storytelling groups in the United States. She helps for- and non-profit organizations around the world identify, hone, capitalize upon, and celebrate their stories. Previous clients include NASA, iRobot Corporation, Dreamfar, Unbound, Quest Diagnostics, and Big Brothers, among many others.

As a coach and teacher, Laura believes her job is to help storytellers, writers, public speakers, and others find their voices and use them effectively. Her supportive and insightful coaching, workshops, and master classes have helped hundreds of people become better storytellers.

Laura is also a sought-after keynote speaker. Her talks are funny, insightful, poignant, and useful, all at once. One event organizer said, "Laura was exactly right for us. She was on target and explained everything in a way we understood and could use. She made us laugh, think, and feel like we were part of the story."

When she isn't telling, Laura writes, enjoys cooking and cycling, loves exploring the world inside and out, and is always open to a new adventure. In recent years, Laura has used the transformative power of writing and story to help her process grief following the 2014 loss of her husband. She has been published in the national press with writings on storytelling, grief, and organizational work.

For her story and more, please visit laurapacker.com, thinkstory.com, and truestorieshonestlies.blogspot.com.

About

Whenever you charge forth to learn and tell a new story, one of the crucial questions you must ask yourself is *What is this story about? What is its meaning?* I'm not talking about the plot but the meaning of the story for both you and the audience. For example, Red Riding Hood is about a girl walking through the woods, disobeying her mother and the consequences thereof, but what is it about? What does it mean culturally? Personally?

When you ask these questions, the meaning changes. Its *about* changes. Is it about the perilous road to adulthood? Asking for help? Stranger danger? What does it mean to you? Why does the story call to you?

Spending some time with these questions will deepen your understanding of the story and therefore deepen your telling. You don't have to explicitly tell the audience what it means (it's often better if you don't) but your understanding will impact the way you tell, what you emphasize, and how you relate to your listeners. It may also change which audiences you tell the story to and the response you expect.

This applies to personal and organizational stories as well as traditional. We must ask our-selves what the *about* is so we understand what we are saying and can craft a thoughtful narrative.

It's worth revisiting the *about* for any story in your repertoire regularly. It may change. I would hope it does change, as you grow and learn more about yourself and the world.

Storytelling is a living art and, as such, we must not fear the deeper work, and the harder questions, asking just what is it all about anyway?

A

Abundance

It's hard to be a working artist or anyone following a calling. It's a constant hustle, always looking for work and always wondering where the next paycheck will come from. For the most part, I manage this well, but there are times when I think I'm nuts. I am *always* working. It's very hard to stop because there isn't as much certainty as there may appear to be in a regular salaried position. I get scared there won't be enough. Enough work, enough money, enough time, enough opportunity. When this happens, I clench up. I fear scarcity.

The solution for me lies in trying to cultivate an attitude of abundance. I'm talking about the belief that there is enough for all of us. When I behave as if the next job will come, the next check won't bounce, the next work will be fulfilling, I am more likely to have that experience.

So many working artists assume scarcity. They assume that work is hard to find and therefore limit the places they are willing to look for it. They assume they won't be paid enough so won't ask for an appropriate fee. This all comes out of fear. The world is a scary place and yes, making a living as an artist is sometimes walking a knife-edge of terror. I fall into this frequently, I'm not trying to suggest I don't, but when I'm lucky and smart, I notice. I take a deep breath. I remind myself there is enough, I just may need to be a little more creative or even redefine what *enough* means. It's up to me to do the work since it's unlikely that success (however I define that) will land on my doorstep if I don't do something to encourage it.

I do several things to create abundance rather than scarcity in my life.

- ◆ **I keep my eyes open.** I am always looking for new opportunities. I don't leave home without business cards. I've gotten gigs from conversations I've had in laundromats, on the bus and in ladies' rooms at the airport. *By being open to opportunity I am assuming the opportunity exists and I will be that much more receptive to it.*
- ◆ **I accept work that is appropriate for me and pass on the work that isn't.** I am an excellent storyteller for many audiences and the right organizational storyteller with many for- and non-profits. But I am not right for every opportunity. If I'm asked to tell stories with little kids, preschoolers, I'd much rather refer a teller who I know loves working with small children and has honed the craft for that audience. Likewise, if someone wants a historical re-enactor. Storytelling requires a great deal of craft and work; none of us are experts at everything. *By passing on work for which I am not suited, I build a stronger internal community and increase our external value, thus building a larger potential audience, since they know they will get the best when they hire a storyteller.*

- **I ask for what I'm worth.** I spend time learning what other performing artists charge and base my rates appropriately. I can always negotiate down; I can't negotiate up. If I charged $50 or $100 for an hour gig that's an hour from home, I'm establishing a low bar at a non-living wage for not only myself but the next storyteller that client wants to hire. *By asking for what I'm worth, I am assuming financial abundance is possible rather than assuming I cannot realistically support myself as an artist.*

- **I keep learning.** I keep trying new things, working on new material, engaging in continuing education and more. *By learning more about my craft, I am assuming I will have the opportunity to practice it.*

- **I remind myself to be grateful for every opportunity, including failure.** When I am grateful for the work, even when it's hard, I remind myself of just how fortunate I am that I make my living doing what I love. *By experiencing and expressing gratitude, it is harder to slip into bitterness when things are tough, so I remain more open to possibility.*

- **I remain passionate about my work.** If I love my work, if I am passionately engaged in my life, I cannot help but experience abundance because each instance of experiencing passion reminds me that more can come. When I talk about my work, that passion is clear, so potential clients know I care about what I do and will give them a better product. I continue to do the work I love. Each time I work I allow myself to love it a little more. *By remaining passionate and loving what I do I cannot help but become better at it and so increase my likelihood of being rehired or recommended.*

We create so many self-fulfilling prophecies in our lives and so often they are negative. Why not try to create some that are positive? If we put as much energy and work into the possibility of hope and abundance as we do into the certainty of loss, maybe our lives will veer just a bit more in the direction we want. Assume abundance while continuing to do the work and see what happens. It's not likely to make things any worse and might just help you live a more joyful and prosperous life.

A

Accents

Let me be very blunt. Unless you have worked with a dialect coach or have the accent yourself, *think deeply and cautiously about using accents*. Assuming an accent and doing it poorly is insulting to the people with that cadence to their speech. Accents differ from character voices, which I address in a separate entry. To be clear, an accent is defined as "a distinctive mode of pronunciation of a language, especially one associated with a particular nation, locality, or social class."

I know some of you are feeling defensive and determined, thinking *but my accents are good and they are important in my stories!*

Please ask yourself these questions:

◆ **Does using the accent add anything to the story that would not be there otherwise?** If, for example, you are telling an Irish story (a kind of story that American tellers often feel the need to accent), what would happen if you told the audience the story was Irish and then told it in your usual intonations? Would the audience think less of you or the story? Isn't your story and your telling good enough without the accent? If the accent adds something crucial to the story maybe you need to look at telling it so the accent is no longer essential.

◆ **What if you told the story in the country whose accent you are borrowing?** Would you use the accent then? If the answer is no, then why are you using an accent elsewhere?

◆ **Do you use accents in all your stories from cultures you are not a part of?** For example, do you tell African stories with an African accent? If you do, is it the one that's appropriate to the language group where the story originated? Do you use regional American accents for each story from the U.S.? If not, then why do you use an accent in some stories and not others?

◆ **Would a person from the culture whose accent you are using know you are not of that culture?** Unless your accent is flawless, it can easily slip into caricature. Is that your intent?

◆ **If you're using an accent in dialogue to differentiate characters, is the dialogue essential?** If you are a white person who has never been to Asia, is it appropriate for you to speak in a generic Asian accent? Could you tell the story so the character is clearly Chinese AND you are not insulting Chinese people by mimicking their speech?

A poorly done accent (and most are poorly done) adds nothing to the story. It may distract the listener from attending as deeply, especially if they are from that culture and know the accent is fake. Accents can also make it difficult to process words and their meaning. You are not serving yourself, the audience, or the story when you add an accent; you may be, in fact, insulting everyone. Even well-done accents add a frequently unnecessary level of complexity to a performance. Your story and performance can stand on their own without accents. You may need to add some introductory context, which can deepen the meaning for the audience, but an accent will rarely enhance.

A

Anecdote or story?

It's hard to tell the difference between an anecdote and a story. At its most basic, an anecdote relates something that happened. A story relates something that happened giving it structure and meaning. While an anecdote may be interesting, sad, amusing, etc., it isn't as likely to stick with your audience or to move them deeply. A story can.

For example, compare these two examples:

The king died. The queen died soon after.
This is an anecdote. It tells you something happened, but no sense of why.

The king died. The queen died soon after of a broken heart.
This is almost a micro story. Something happened and then something else happened in response.

Stories have structure and conflict. There is a beginning, middle, and end; something happens that produces a response which produces another response.

You might have a great anecdote about the time you fell out of a boat in the middle of the rapids. You might tell it and people are scared, thrilled, delighted that you are here to tell it to them. It becomes a story when you give it some context (who were you with, where were you) and offer a conclusion other than your survival (how you were changed by the experience).

There is a place for anecdotes; they are common in daily conversation and easily can be woven into speeches or formal presentations. Just make sure you aren't telling an anecdote thinking it's a story. Your audience will be more satisfied with their listening experience if you give them a strong emotional story arc that goes somewhere.

Applied storytelling

Storytelling is a basic part of what it is to be human, so it can and should be used in a wide range of settings. While most people think of "performance" when they hear *storytelling*, it can be used in almost any situation where people are gathered, information and meaning must be conveyed, and community is being built.

While none of these examples are comprehensive, here are some uses of applied storytelling:

♦ **Educators** use storytelling to teach or enhance lessons in a wide range of topics. For example, a science teacher can tell a story about the discovery of a theory (e.g., DNA) to humanize it, or they can use a traditional story to illustrate a concept (e.g., a creation story as a metaphor for certain geological concepts).

♦ **Legal** professionals must be able to craft and tell compelling stories as part of their arguments. **Medical** professionals also need to be good at explaining complex ideas simply, and they must be superb listeners, a basic storytelling skill.

♦ **Clergy members from any faith** may use storytelling to help their parishioners understand theological or moral concepts. They may also use stories when they offer counsel.

♦ **Organizational storytelling** is the application of storytelling in organizational settings, usually for- and non-profit organizations. Most typically, organizational storytelling is used in conjunction with human resources (to attract the right people, to boost morale, etc.); leadership (to navigate through change, to build relationships, etc.); marketing, branding, and external communications (find the right stories to talk about products and services, using story to discuss organizational issues externally, etc.); internal communications (internal branding, navigating change, etc.); and in other facets of organizational work.

♦ **Product development and design storytelling** use narrative tools to build the right product for a focused group of customers or works to ensure the products are easily usable.

♦ **Social justice** can use storytelling as a powerful way to build empathy and compassion by telling stories about specific people affected by social injustice. Issues of racism, sexism, or other social ills become much more meaningful when they can be personified by their impact on an individual. The listening tools used by many storytellers can also be used in social justice work to break down barriers between people. Stories also provide tools for representation; by telling stories with a wide range of characters, storytellers can subtly remind their listeners that representation matters.

A

◆ **Therapeutic storytelling** is part of several therapeutic methodologies, including narrative and exposure therapies. By telling our stories, we can build new understandings of who we are and how we function. Please be aware; narrative therapy differs from telling a difficult story in performance. The latter should happen only once it has been thoroughly processed, in therapy or elsewhere.

Applied storytelling capitalizes on our basic human need for story and on the neurology that makes it such an effective way to evoke empathy, understanding, and learning.

Appropriation

Appropriation in storytelling means the act of telling stories from a culture or way of being that is not yours. This typically applies to someone telling a traditional or sacred story when they are not of that culture. Each storyteller you ask will have a different opinion about this, so what follows are my personal guidelines. Search your own heart to see what works for you.

Some storytellers believe that all stories belong to all people. While I believe we can learn from all stories, I don't think all stories are okay for all people to tell. Stories from cultural groups who have been marginalized, whose stories have been stolen from them, are not stories I choose to tell. An example would be a story sacred to a Native American tribe. I am a white woman whose family immigrated to the United States in the early part of the 20th century. Part of the privilege I experience and the comfort I live in is directly related to the horrors Native Americans were and are subjected to. Sometimes, the stories are all a tribe may have remaining. They are not mine to tell.

Equally, I will not tell stories of the African American experience in the first person. I might tell a story of this experience in the third person, or clearly from the perspective of a white person, but it would be appropriation were I to tell such a tale in the first person. Nor would I tell first-person stories about specific pieces of the histories of disenfranchised people, because I did not experience the events and I am not a member of that oppressed group. I might tell a story from the viewpoint of someone who changed their mind because of those events.

Appropriation may not always be clear. For instance, call and response storytelling is a form of storytelling that has grown out of African story and song traditions. It is a participatory form of storytelling that requires responses from the audience when the storyteller utters a particular phrase. Traditionally, this has built a connection between audience and teller; assuring the teller that the audience is still engaged, and creating a dialogue between all parties. Is it cultural appropriation for a white person to tell a story with call and response? I'm not sure, but I know it falls to the storyteller to research, ask questions, determine if this call and response has sacred meaning, and decide. Don't just assume it's okay.

Many traditional stories fall into such hazy places; each storyteller must make up her own mind about it. It's possible to take concerns about appropriation to an extreme and end up with nothing you can tell outside of your own life, so here are some guidelines I follow.

A

- **I do some research.** Is the story a sacred tale? More importantly, is the story sacred in the culture from which it originated, whether or not I consider it sacred? If it is, I then have two choices. If I know the story is widely told in my culture, I decide if I want to tell it. A good example of this might be an Anansi tale. I ask myself how I would feel if someone told a similar story I find sacred or highly specific to my culture or way of being. If I do want to tell it, I craft it with as much cultural relevance and respect as I can. When I tell it I *always* give it context so the listeners hear not only the story but gain an understanding of its importance.

- If my research tells me this story is still sacred, is still used in sacred ways, or is not a part of the common vernacular, I stop. It isn't my story to tell. Again, consider how you might feel if someone took the stories most sacred to you and told it out of context without believing it. That might make you uncomfortable.

- **If I have decided to tell the story, I get three sources** to determine that it is, in fact, a traditional story in the public domain. Many festivals and other storytelling venues ask their tellers to verify traditional material with three sources, so it's a good habit to develop.

- **On the rare occasions I feel overwhelmingly drawn to tell a living sacred story**, I contact appropriate representatives of the culture from which it comes, usually elders, preferably storytellers. I approach them respectfully and talk with them about the story, about why I feel so strongly drawn to tell it. I do the work to ensure that the story remains sacred. Sometimes I've been told yes, I may tell the story. When that happens, each time I tell it, I give as much context as I can and I express my gratitude. Sometimes I've been told no. When that has happened, the story leaves my repertoire. Period. It isn't mine to tell. To the best of my ability, I will not engage in cultural appropriation. There are so many stories in the world. Surely I can find another that will work for me.

I have certainly made mistakes but these guidelines generally work for me. I know the stories I tell are mine to tell. I know I am not stealing anyone else's work, that it is my own intellectual property, and that I am being respectful of other cultures. It's not a lot of work, when you get down to it, to make sure you aren't stealing, defiling, or blaspheming.

Audience

Effective storytelling is a dance between teller, audience, and tale; this dance is especially visible in performance storytelling. Storytelling is also an act of service. If you approach your audience with service and relationship in mind, and remember that it is your job to engage them, not their obligation to be engaged, you have a better chance of being more effective. Likewise, the audience is not there to serve you; you need to be sure that your stories are practiced and crafted, so at no point will the audience be removed from their own experience of the story to worry about you.

◆ **Who is your audience?** It helps if you know who your audience is and what stories are appropriate for them. Meet them at least half-way and give them a chance to engage with you. If it turns out that the audience is radically different than what you expected (you were told it would be all adults expecting scary Halloween stuff and you're looking at a room full of preschoolers whom you don't want to traumatize) do your best to modify your set to match their needs. It's worth talking to the organizer afterward, but your first concern is that you meet the needs of the audience.

◆ **The audience is not your therapist.** I have seen otherwise powerful stories ruined by the storyteller expecting the audience to take care of them, breaking into heart-felt sobs or otherwise not managing their own emotions. It's okay to have feelings while you tell a story, but do not leave the audience wondering if you are or will be okay. That isn't the job of the audience: their job is to listen and appreciate the story. It's your job to hone your story and craft it so you won't ask the audience for care beyond the bounds of being an attentive audience.

◆ **What do they expect?** What are they expecting to hear? They are giving you the gift of their attention because they are anticipating particular things from you. Do your best to meet and exceed those expectations. Sometimes, it's appropriate to subvert those expectations, but even then, do so to improve and enhance their experience.

◆ **Does size matter?** We all want good-sized audiences. It's easy to see value in a large audience, knowing I have drawn a whole bunch of people to my show. It can be harder to see value in smaller but still deeply appreciative audiences because the immediate visual hit of fewer people in the room is unsettling.

I am reminded of what my storytelling mentor Brother Blue used to say, "*The room is full of angels.*" Regardless of the size of the audience, if they are present, interested and engaged, then it is a good audience. It feels good when there are more people and there is something about a critical mass that helps good storytelling become better, but the key is the connection between teller and listener, be that one child utterly entranced by a story, ten adults having a really good time or a thousand each in their own shared moment. It's about remembering that every individual audience member has chosen to be there and you are honoring their presence by doing the best you can.

You may be able to mitigate the feeling that an audience is too small by inviting them to come closer or by arranging the seats to encourage them to sit together, rather than scattered through the room.

◆ **Love them where they are.** If you love the audience in their current state, then you are likely to be more able to connect with them. When we love our audiences and recognize that they are no different from us beyond the fact that we are on the stage and they are our listeners, we can't help but want to do our best for them. We can't help but want to invite them into the shared experience of storytelling.

◆ **Foster connection.** Be present. Look at your audience. Meet them where they are. Be grateful for their attention and presence with you. Invite them into the story. Because it's so easy to forgo the theatrical boundary of the fourth wall in storytelling, you have a powerful opportunity to include them in the story creation process, so welcome them in and let them know that you are as grateful for them as they are for you.

Authenticity

There is a lot of blather about authenticity out there. Gurus tell us we will be happier if we *live an authentic life* but what does that mean?

I view an authentic life (and an authentic *artistic* life) as one where I strive to make choices that align with my values, with my vision of who I want to be (though I'm not likely to ever get there). I strive for awareness of how my behavior impacts the world and others. I strive (at a minimum) to be honest about who I am and my intentions.

For me, as both a storyteller and a human being, authenticity comes down to a few basic precepts.

◆ **Understand my own values and understand that they will change.** I keep a list in my journal of the values that matter the most. I re-examine it occasionally to see if anything has changed. Things do change from time to time because we change. Knowing my values gives me guideposts in everything I do.

    As a storyteller, knowing my own values helps me choose material, select gigs, and engage with audiences.

◆ **Be honest with myself.** This means examining my motives; noticing when I'm being inauthentic and asking why; examining why I react as I do to different stimuli.

    As a storyteller, radical self-honesty helps me understand why a given story matters to me, what it says about me and my work, and the inner forces that drive me to tell it in a certain way.

◆ **Strive for honesty with others.** Everyone lies. Avoid it when you can. Lying creates cognitive dissonance as we try to reconcile the falsehood with the truth. We all are boring, small-minded, and greedy. While I don't like admitting this about myself, it helps me avoid situations where I might want to lie.

    As a storyteller, this means that, whether I'm telling a fictional story or (especially when) I'm telling a true one, I aim for emotional honesty. The story must be authentic with my experience in the world.

◆ **Fail again. Fail better.** I fail all the time. Maybe every day. If I'm failing, I'm risking. Sometimes those risks lead to amazing things. I try to redefine failure, so instead of berating myself for failure I instead ask what I can learn from the experience. What parts worked?

    As a storyteller, I don't want to rely on the tried and true. I want to learn new things, try new kinds of art, and share them with my audience, so it's inevitable that not everything will be as well executed as I'd like. If I allow for periods of growth and trial, if I accept that some things won't work and plan for it, it's easier to try again. This helps me to be more authentic because I'm more willing to risk something new and grow.

◆ **Trust myself.** If I understand my motives, values, and remain honest with myself then I can trust myself to make decisions that support motives and values.

As a storyteller, that means I will make better choices about the gigs I accept and the work I do.

◆ **Trust my audience.** When I trust my audience, I can more readily build a relationship with them. This leads to a more authentic experience.

◆ **Be open. Risk openness.** This leads to more authentic experiences because I engage with the world with less pretense.

The same thing applies to storytelling. When I am open to the story, to my audience, to the process, I experience it more fully and can reflect it back with more authenticity.

◆ **Be kind. Be kind. Be kind.** Be kind to myself. Be kind to others. Be kind to the world. This is probably my core value. Be kind. When I operate from a base of kindness, I become more forgiving, more loving, more able to see the world as one of possibility and hope. It is then more possible to be vulnerable in all I do, story-related or not.

To be more authentic.

To be. And being is the core of authenticity.

Backstory

Webster's defines backstory as *a narrative providing a history or background context, especially for a character or situation in a literary work, film, or dramatic series.* This includes storytelling.

Storytellers should have a sense of what happened before the starting point of their story and after the end. Before *Once upon a time*, after *Happily ever after.* You need not tell the audience the backstory (in fact, it might be detrimental and distracting were you to do so) but it may very well inform how you tell the story.

Let's look at a familiar story and see how backstory might influence the ways you tell it.

Think about Little Red Riding Hood for a moment, the version you know best. Remind yourself of the beginning, the middle and the end. If it's already in your repertoire think about how you feel when you start to tell it, your body language, your expressions, and stance.

Now ask yourself some questions about what happened before the start of the story and about the world the story lives in. You don't have to answer all of them, maybe only one or two.

- How old is the little girl? How old is the mother?
- Why is there no father on the scene?
- Can they afford the goodies they are sending to the grandmother?
- Does the grandmother have something the mother or granddaughter wants?
- Does the mother like/love the grandmother? Is the grandmother the mother's mother or the father's mother?
- Does the girl like/love the grandmother?
- How often does the girl visit her grandmother? Is the path familiar?
- Is it a sunny day? A cloudy one? Morning? Evening?
- Is the path clear or is it obscured?
- Why did the grandmother make the cloak red?
- How long has she been sick? Is she very sick? Is she faking it for attention?
- Is the wolf starving? Bored? Horny?
- Do all animals talk in this world?

B

You get the idea. I know this is a lot of questions, probably too many for one story and one example, but answering even a few might change your understanding of the story and may shape how you convey that meaning to the audience.

Another of my favorite ways to develop backstory and therefore deepen my understanding of the story is interviewing. I get together with a trusted friend, one whom I know is interested in helping me be a better artist, and I tell them just a little bit about the story I'm working on. I give them a general outline of events and characters. Then I select one of the characters and invite them to ask me questions as if they were interviewing the character.

I do this only with trusted allies because I need to know I won't be interrupted while I answer and that they will let me think my answers through. The interviewer needs to let the subject remain in charge of the interview.

Once the ground rules are set, we begin. Typical questions might include:

◆ What is your name? Why were you named that?
◆ Do you have any siblings?
◆ Who was your best friend when you were young?
◆ What do you think of so-and-so (another character from the story)?
◆ What makes you happy?
◆ Do you have any career goals?

Sometimes you'll uncover something that might be a real story-changer or may lead you to a new story entirely, a piece of backstory you didn't expect. My first-person telling of Hansel and Gretel from the witch's perspective came out of one of these exercises. This technique extends far beyond traditional material. Try it with a personal story or something from the public domain. It can get silly, but it almost always yields new information about the character or story.

Once you know some of the backstory you can weave that understanding into how you tell the story. It might impact the imagery you use when talking about the forest or wolf. It might change your body language when you talk about the grandmother sick in bed. The possibilities are endless. Examining the backstory might even suggest a whole new way to tell the story. You may not need to share this information with your audience but it might change how you present a character or a situation. For instance, did you know the Big Bad Wolf used to keep kosher?

Baggage

I don't know about you, but I have a deluxe engraved luggage set. I received the first piece when I was very small and have been adding to it steadily ever since. While it's not terribly practical – I can't carry anything in it – and it's heavy, it is at once one of my most guarded and hated possessions.

You know what I'm talking about, of course. It's not real luggage but the baggage we all carry, simply from having been born into a world and into families populated with other human beings. We acquire wounds, scars, habits and more that can weigh us down, hence baggage. All of this has an impact on our whole lives, including our storytelling lives.

As a storyteller and an artist, I find it worthwhile to remember this. If I'm struggling with a story; if I resist a certain kind of audience; if I get grumpy about a work task, it's useful if I ask myself why? Sometimes it will be only that I'm tired. Other times may be the person who hired me is vaguely like that kid who bullied me in grade school, so old patterns and reflexes are at play. Or maybe now is not the time for me to attend a performance based on something triggering for me.

Understanding our own baggage gives us a chance to live more fully realized lives. Knowing that I simply dislike certain aspects of my work is useful. Recognizing that I am reminded of something challenging by something innocuous helps me moderate my responses. And knowing that an experience may have lasting repercussions gives me a chance to choose if I want to engage in it and pay the cost.

If we take the time to ask ourselves why we are drawn to or repelled by a part of our storytelling lives (or any part of our whole lives), we can make better choices. We can undertake a task knowing it will be challenging. We can try to put down some of our baggage. We can let an opportunity go, knowing it will have a significant impact on our internal lives. None of these responses are unreasonable if we have a sense of who we are and what we bring with us to the experience; none of these responses are unethical if we make them quickly enough that it won't adversely affect organizers, performers, or audiences.

We all have baggage. We don't have to be controlled by it most of the time though there will always be times when we carry the whole set and don't even realize it. A little mindfulness can help. By living a mindful life and least looking for and understanding potential triggers, we can become artists with greater authenticity, humans who are more honest with ourselves and those around us, and create a world that is more connected, more interesting and more supportive of who we are and our work.

Beginnings

B

The start of your story is the doorway. It gives you a chance to set audience expectations, which you then can support or subvert as you see fit. It's important to remember that the beginning of your story isn't when you open your mouth, it's in the moments before, when you connect with your listeners and let them know by body language and attitude they can trust you, they can relax and come along for the ride.

What do you do when you first walk onto a stage or other performance venue? Many novice tellers rush right into their story, without taking a moment to greet the audience and assess the space around them. When you're not comfortable with telling, with the material or with the environment, you may find yourself diving right in without taking a moment to say hello. This may lead to your story sounding rushed or the audience losing the first few beats of the telling because they didn't have a chance to focus their attention. If you do this, you're not alone. We all rush into the telling sometimes without taking a moment to be present.

When we rush into telling because we're nervous or concerned we won't have enough time, several things happen. You don't have a chance to look around and develop a sense of who is in front of you and what space you're working with. The audience doesn't have a chance to look at you before they must concentrate on listening. They need a moment to get used to you. By taking just a moment to gather yourself together and for the audience to see you, it's much easier to build rapport and connection.

Next time you're about to perform, take a moment before you launch into your performance. You can do this without it appearing forced in several ways.

Walk to the mic or telling space then:

◆ pause and smile at the audience.
◆ take a breath then begin your story.
◆ fiddle with the mic to ensure it's in the right place.
◆ develop a signature way of greeting your audience or starting stories. I often walk on stage and say "good evening" (whatever is appropriate for the time of day) or "thank you."

It may feel very vulnerable, letting the audience see you before you launch into your performance, but vulnerability is part of what makes good storytelling. It allows the audience to feel more connected with you and gives them permission to be vulnerable in turn. Taking just that moment to acknowledge them, to settle into the moment and to give yourself a chance to breathe means your performance will be more centered, more powerful and more connected.

Once you have said hello and established to your audience that you will take care of them, they can dive into the images and narrative you give them.

From there, the beginning of your story establishes setting, character, genre and other vital narrative components. Your beginning gives your listeners a clue as to what they're in for.

"Once upon a time…"

"It was a dark and stormy night…"

"Thank you for inviting me to speak with you about my work…"

"When I was a little girl…"

"A dog, a cat, and an elephant walk into a bar…"

"Everyone expects their child to be born perfect. Sometimes we need to change what perfect means…"

Each of these beginnings sets an expectation. You must quickly give your listeners enough information so they at least *think* they know where the story is going. This lets them relax and build their own relationship with the narrative, so crucial in any storytelling experience. You then can stick with expected direction or not. It's up to you.

Those first few moments of the story, the beginning moments, are the vital time when you build a relationship with the audience, start off in a direction they can relate to, and remind yourself that yes, you know what you're doing.

Blocks and motivation

I was teaching an introductory storytelling class and one student asked, "What do you do when it just won't work? When the story won't come together? Is there a storytelling equivalent of writer's block?" What an excellent question!

Yes, I have found there is a storyteller's equivalent of writer's block. There are times when I am working on a story and just can't find the right words or the right hook to connect with the audience. There are other times when I just don't have the motivation for work and want to have a tantrum.

We have all hit that place where we don't want to do *that* gig, deal with *that* producer or when we feel as though we can't. It's a tough place to be because really, all we want to do is give in, have the tantrum and eat some chocolate. At least that's what I want.

Here are some of the things I've done that help me get past troublesome moments in story crafting, performance, and in finding the motivation to do some of the more tedious work involved in being a working artist.

◆ **Ask myself why I'm having the problem.** Am I ready to tell this story? Are there big emotions attached to it that I need to sort through before I can tell it? Do I like the story? Is it interesting?

◆ **Kill my darlings.** Writers are frequently told they "must kill their darlings," meaning writers must be wary of the pieces of their own work they most treasure. This applies to storytellers, too. I don't mean we shouldn't love our stories and characters, but we need to be careful that we don't use the same tropes without ceasing. We may also become so attached to a character or scene that we refuse to allow the work to change or grow. We may also be so enamored with a bit of craft that we don't notice it has little to do with the story or may be distracting to the audience. Darling bits may obscure the actual storyline, may inhibit your ability to connect with the audience and may be redundant. When I'm stuck, I will take a hard look at the piece and ask myself if I need to remove the parts I most adore. I'll try it and see what happens next.

◆ **Turn it inside out.** What would happen if I told the story from a different viewpoint or started at the end and told it backward? What if I made the hero the villain? This may get me around the trouble spots or, at a minimum, I will learn more about the story and its meaning.

◆ **Minimize then regrow.** Sometimes I'll try to tell a story in six words. *Red cloaks won't stop the wolves.* When I do, I'm forced to pick only the most crucial elements. *Cursed* *sleep now, insomnia ever after.* Once I've done a few six-word versions. I'll then try telling it again and see if I can move beyond the stuck parts. *Pigs flunk out of architecture school.*

◆ **Give it a break.** If I'm having a tough time I may go for a walk, read something unrelated, cook, clean, work on a different piece. To make sure this doesn't lapse into procrastination, I will set a timer or schedule my next work session for the piece.

◆ **Remind myself why I love the craft.** This is another kind of break. I will sometimes stop what I'm working on and listen to another storyteller, one whose work I admire. Listening to them might frustrate me or it might inspire me to try again with renewed enthusiasm. Alternatively, I'll give myself an artist's date, an exercise pioneered in *The Artist's Way* by Julia Cameron. I'll go to a museum and spend 15 minutes looking at one piece of art. I'll listen to music with no other distraction. I'll find some way to remind me of the value of art and storytelling.

◆ **Approach it through a different art.** I keep a pad of construction paper and a box of crayons handy. At some point when I'm working on a story, I will often draw out scenes using stick figures and a few speech bubbles. This makes me get away from the words and concentrate on the images instead.

◆ **Am I too isolated?** Am I lonely? Do I need support? How long has it been since I got some appreciation? Do I need to phone a friend and get a pep talk? Do I need a hug? If I am in a place where there are no local storytellers to listen to me, I may call a friend or go online for support.

◆ **Is the problem physical?** Am I tired, hungry, thirsty? Am I in pain? Would taking a nap, eating, drinking, or an analgesic help?

◆ **Is there a problem with the project?** Do I think it's somehow unethical, inauthentic, or inappropriate for me? Does it involve someone I find troubling? What can I do about this, or is it just a lesson to be learned?

◆ **Is it resistance and self-sabotage?** Am I fighting my own best interests because some part of me believes I am not worthy? Am I afraid no one will care about the work? If so, how can I remind myself that what I do matters and is meaningful?

◆ **Sometimes I just need to take a deep breath and keep going.** If I encounter a block when on stage, I will take a moment. I'll take a deep breath and keep going. That little pause is usually enough to help me through the difficult moment, to remember the lost line, to reconnect with the audience.

We all will have times when we don't want to do something or feel blocked. We all have times when we feel ineffective or scared. We need to remember that we are not alone in this work, we can remind ourselves of what we love about it, and that when we step up and do it, it will mean something to someone. We must remember to be kind to ourselves as we do the hard work of making art.

Bookings

If you love your work, you want to work, but how do you get bookings? Volumes are written on this topic and many guarantee their effectiveness and ease, but I can't promise that. Getting bookings requires ongoing, hard work.

Here are some tools and resources I use to generate bookings. None are foolproof.

◆ **Ask.** If you know someone who might be able to book you in front of the audiences you want, ask. For example, if someone you know has a venue, ask them if they would like to book you. If you have teacher friends, ask them if you can tell in their classrooms. Don't be shy or wait for them to ask you.

◆ **Read books** like *Book Yourself Solid* by Michael Port. Use the methods they recommend and see what works for you.

◆ **Always have business cards with you.** When people discover you're a storyteller they often want to know more.

◆ **Have effective social media profiles** on services such as Facebook, LinkedIn, Twitter, Instagram, etc. Be selective about which you will use; you can spend your whole life keeping up on social media, so pick a max of two or three and focus on them.

  Facebook, Twitter, and other social media ads can be highly effective or a bust. It's worth running some low-budget tests to see what kinds get the most response.

◆ **Go to events**, not just as a teller but as an audience member. This functions not only as community building but also as continuing education.

◆ **Postcard campaigns** can be effective but require a lot of follow up. It's not enough to send out postcards, you will need to reach out afterward.

◆ **Booking services** such as gigsalad.com may lead to work. Free profiles are limited but can get you something.

◆ **Be careful with freebies.** Yes, you want to give things away hoping it will lead to work, but too much free work and you will have no paid gigs at all. I talk more about this in compensation. If you have materials, such as books, pens, recordings, etc., budget a certain amount to be given away.

◆ **Return phone calls and emails promptly.** I cannot stress this enough. The early bird often gets the worm.

◆ **Set a marketing schedule**, so you know what you're working on, when, who you're targeting, and why.

Boundaries

When I began storytelling, I told fairy tales with little embellishment or interpretation. Pretty quickly I moved toward radical reinterpretations of the same material, then original fiction and occasionally personal stories. I began to experiment with non-linear narrative, multiple point-of-view stories and taboo issues (sexuality and death, in particular). Remember, this was 25+ years ago when most people told traditional material or mild personal stories, so what I was doing was avant-garde and quite challenging for many listeners. I know that now sexuality and creative narrative forms are common, but then? Not so much.

I was experimenting and growing, and I loved it. I had found an art form that suited me where I could explore and expand. My community supported my creativity and was willing to give me a pretty long rope to play with. I was careful about what I told to whom, where and when I tried more radical material. I paid attention to my audiences' needs while still feeding my own need for experimentation and creativity.

A few years into my telling career, a beloved older mentor pulled me aside and told me I had to reign it in. That I was offending people. That I didn't dress well so I was insulting my audience. That my stories were largely inappropriate for any listener. She told me I had tremendous talent and gifts but that I was abusing them and my audience. Remember, I was in my mid-twenties; *no one else* was telling material like this, and she was one of the community pillars.

I believed her.

I immediately went back to strict interpretations of traditional tales and very little else. I acquired what seemed to be the appropriate wardrobe. I shrank and began to wonder if my stories were worth telling at all. I thought no one wanted to hear my voice.

It was awful. For about a year I tried to fit in. I failed. I'm glad I failed.

Eventually, I concluded that she was expressing her own discomfort with my stories and there had to be an audience that would like them. I began to seek out new venues and build my own audiences. I started venues, went to places where storytelling wasn't the norm, expanded beyond my boundaries. It was hard work, but worth it. I regained my voice. I again told and continue to tell a wide range of material. Some of it's challenging, some of it isn't, but it's all mine and it's all work I relish.

B

It's hard to be an artist who stretches boundaries, regardless of the art form. It requires a willingness to make others uncomfortable and to take the risk that some people won't like you. David Bowie is one of my personal heroes when I think about boundaries and expectations. If he found a boundary, he pushed against it, and eventually became a role-model for so many of us struggling to find our own selves and own voices. When I was struggling to rediscover my authentic voice after that well-meaning but misguided advice, David Bowie was one of the people I looked to. If he could do it and so much more dramatically than I was, I could do it too.

The only thing I now regret about following my own passion for boundary-pushing work is that for a little while I believed someone who told me I was too much, that what I was doing was too extreme. I still push against boundaries. I'm sure I have a better sense of appropriate time, place and audience now than I did when I was in my mid-twenties, but when I see a boundary, I tend to run at it. Honestly, this is one of the themes of my whole life. There is certainly a cost – for example, most people don't know I can tell a fine fairy tale appropriate for anyone, so I don't get the bookings I might want – but it's a cost I've chosen to pay.

Do the work that calls to you. Be smart about it, choose where and when to share it. For instance, I don't tell sexy stories to kids. I do tell them to consenting adults who know what to expect in a given show, some of which contain dirty words. Share your work with the world. We need to push against boundaries, those we build for ourselves and those the world imposes.

Storytelling is so powerful because it's essentially a direct brain-to-brain connection. As storytellers, we open new worlds to our listeners. We are the explorers, the cartographers, the preachers, the scientists, and the dreamers. So sometimes our work frightens others. Do it anyway. Break the boundaries and see what lies beyond. If you love strict interpretations of fairy tales, tell them. If you love historical work that challenges commonly held beliefs, pursue it. If you need to tell your truth, then tell it as it stands. If you need to sing and dance and cry out to the sky as you tell, then sing and dance and ululate. Find your audiences. Tell your tale. Live the work.

Character

Compared to writers, performing storytellers have some interesting advantages and challenges when presenting characters. There are an endless number of character tips I could give you, but I will limit myself to a few I use in almost every practice, almost every writing session, almost every performance.

Like writers, we must know our characters inside and out, far beyond what we present to our audiences. What motivates them? What do they care about? What are their flaws, virtues, hidden vices, and secret dreams? Why are they doing what they're doing? You can find many online resources for character questions, a quick search with a phrase like *character questions* will give you extensive lists.

If we know the answers to these questions and more, then we have more flexibility in how we portray our characters. It doesn't matter if your characters are fiction, traditional, or real; the better you know them, the more believable they will be. Your portrayal will have depth. Even if you are telling a true story, it helps if you imagine some of these answers. Just make them consistent with what you know about the characters in your story. For example:

◆ Did Eleanor Roosevelt have allergies? This might be relevant if your story is set in the spring of 1944.
◆ How does Anansi keep his shoes organized? Maybe Coyote's fur itches?
◆ Even if you can't ask her, decide what made your great-grandmother laugh.

Everyone, whether living or dead, real or fictional, is composed of the details of their lives. Don't tell us, but you certainly can show us some of the details with body language, phrasing, and inflection.

Do your research. If your character is a firefighter, spend time learning about the trade. What's more, as a performing storyteller, learn something about how firefighters hold themselves, how they move, the look in their eyes when they talk about a particularly tough spot. Writers must do all this through words alone; as storytellers, we can use our bodies and voices to convey additional detail to our audiences. That detail should be authentic, so do your homework.

When you portray a character before an audience, be consistent. If you develop a unique voice or physical characteristic, do it each time we meet that character. The audience will come to depend on those cues to know who they are seeing and listening to. If you can't be consistent, then don't do it.

C

Lastly, fall in love with your characters, even the villains. If you love them, you will know them better, portray them with more authenticity and enjoy spending time with them. Your love for the characters gives your audience permission to feel for them too, whether love or disgust. Your passion will be expressed in your words and gestures; your characters will come to life.

Character voices

A character voice differs from an accent. You are changing your pitch, modulation or otherwise altering your speech to represent a character. Please note, this is not permission to use an accent to represent a character, this can quickly fall into parody and is discussed in the accents entry. Characters can have distinct voices to help you and the audience distinguish one from the other.

Some things to think about when you use a character voice:

◆ Can you do the voice consistently, every time that character speaks?
◆ Remember, it's the character's voice, so you must be able to stop using it when you move back to narration (anytime you're not speaking in their voice specifically).
◆ Will the voice hurt your vocal cords?
◆ Do you have more than one character voice? I know a male storyteller who voices every single female character with the same voice. It gets confusing and can be inadvertently insulting.
◆ Is there body language that might accompany that voice? Can you do that consistently?
◆ How else can you differentiate one character from another?
◆ What does the character voice add to the telling? If you use a speech impediment (a lisp, for example) to distinguish the character, are you using it appropriately?

If you use character voices, please practice them. Get listened to and get help making sure they are consistent, individual, and not insulting. A well-done character voice can add immensely to the story; a poorly one will only detract and distract.

Coaching

A good storytelling coach can help you become a much better storyteller. When someone with a good sense of story, a compassionate ear, and the right training listens to you, they may be able to give you the guidance you need to take your storytelling to the next level.

Coaching can be short or long term. Some people use coaches to help them with a singular project, while others have a coach as a long-term ally. It's up to you and your needs.

There are many storytelling coaches available. I would suggest you listen to them tell, take a workshop with them if you can (many coaches teach at conferences), and have a good conversation with them about their methods to make sure that you will work well together. It may take a little while to find the right rhythm, so give it a little time; equally, don't be afraid to state your needs, including if you think they may not be the right coach for you.

An alternative to hiring a coach is to form a peer coaching group, where you and a handful of your colleagues work on stories together. I would highly encourage you to set down ground rules for peer coaching, including what kind of feedback is acceptable, how to set limits, and under what circumstances someone might be asked to leave the group. It is critical that you always let the person being coached state their needs, and that the peers are gentle in their critique. A new story, or one being reworked, is rather like a toddler and needs encouragement rather than harsh criticism.

You may feel called to coach, to help others with their storytelling. I would suggest that you get coached by a variety of coaches before you coach others. Note what you find effective and what is not effective. You may also want to pursue specific training in how to coach, starting with effective listening and praise. If you decide to coach others, don't forget to tell them what they can expect from a coaching session, and to do the best you can to encourage them, support them, and help them make their story and performance their own.

Compensation

Artists deserve to be paid for their work. I could write an entire book about compensation but will instead give you some general guidelines and recommendations. I have touched upon some of this in ethics so look there too.

◆ **Why should I charge for my work?** Because you and your art are worth something. Money is the metaphor we use to connote value; we value that which we pay for, and we know we are valued when we are paid.

In a greater setting, we must charge for our work because we are members of a larger community of storytellers and the still larger community of artists. By charging for our work, we are saying that not only does our individual work have value, but so does the work of other artists. We are saying art matters and is worth investing in.

Finally, you aren't charging just for the performance itself. You are charging for your experience, the time you put into developing the work, your transportation costs and more.

◆ **How much should I charge?** How much you should charge varies widely, based on where you live, how experienced you are, what you have been asked to do and more. Talk with people in your community; talk with other storytellers and discover what they charge. I know this might be challenging. Money is a taboo topic. By talking about it we lessen the taboo and may even help each other.

I've had the experience of moving into a new community several times; one of the things I try to do early on is talk with other artists and set my rates to be aligned with theirs. I don't want to charge too much more or too much less.

◆ **Won't I get more work if I charge less than everyone else? Who will hire me if I charge that much?** Do you want to be the person who everyone knows charges less and sucks up all the work? Do you want to be that tired and isolated? Sure, you might get more work but you will be diminishing your community, your relationships, and likely your prosperity too. You might charge less and have more gigs, but you'll be running yourself ragged and burning bridges behind you. By making your rates more-or-less in alignment with other storytellers you are reinforcing the truth that arts are worth paying for.

You may have to negotiate your rates some, but most people and organizations understand that your time is valuable; this is called *perceived value*. People assume something that costs too little is of lower quality. Think about it. Imagine you are booking a band for your wedding. Do you want to hire the cheapest band that maybe only knows one song and can't play it well? Would you prefer the band that did five gigs yesterday and is exhausted today? Wouldn't you rather hire the right band that has a broad repertoire, is excited to play for you, and can help everyone have fun? Hiring a storyteller is no different.

C

◆ **They say it will be great exposure if I do it for free.** And we all can die of exposure. If you work for free, do so with no expectations. They may promise you a million referrals but there is no guarantee those will come through.

Personally, if it's a cause I'm passionate about and I want to donate my time, I still give them an invoice with my full rate noted, so they don't have the expectation that anyone else will work for free or that I will next time. I see if I can negotiate an ad in the program book or if they will print up programs so listeners have my contact information. There are events that may not pay much AND are good exposure or experience (some arts festivals, for example) but do those knowing your finances will take a hit and you may never see any more work for it.

I don't work for free often because the non-monetary costs are too great. Transportation is still expensive, the time spent in prep could have been used looking for paid work, I may get another offer for paid work in the same time but I've already committed to the free work, and I know when I work for free, I am setting an expectation that other storytellers will also work for free.

◆ **What about pro bono work?** You may want to donate your services to something you care about. That differs from working for exposure. If you do this, make sure the organizers understand this is an in-kind donation. Give them an invoice with your usual rates on it and a note that it is discounted. (I am not a tax professional; some people say you can write these off as a charitable donation. Please don't take my word for it.)

As you can see, compensation is a complex topic. Talk with other storytellers. Look for basic business resources to learn about invoicing or what to do when you don't get paid. Don't be afraid to ask questions and most of all, remember, your work is valuable. Being paid does not diminish the value or purity of your art.

Context, the external world around every performance

Performing and applied storytellers must always be aware of the context within which they work. This includes not only the physical space and the audience but the weather, the news, the community and more.

A story that was appropriate a week ago may no longer be a good choice. For example, some years ago I was helping to program a storytelling festival. One performer was invited to tell a piece about the Triangle Shirtwaist Factory fire, an early industrial accident that helped shape industrial safety standards. In the story, he described the fire in some detail and the choice many of the young workers faced: die in flame and smoke or jump out of a seventh story window to possible safety. We invited him to tell this story in the summer, for a festival that happened in October. It was a good story and a good choice, until September. This story takes place in 2001, and by October 2001 any story of people leaping from a tall building to escape smoke and flame had a very different meaning than earlier. Because of the events of September 11th, 2001, the context of the world changed. Fortunately, the teller had other stories in his repertoire.

Most contextual choices will not be this dramatic but be aware of what's happening around you. Is it hot and the room is stuffy? Listeners might be more likely to doze off so you might change the program to include some participatory tales. Are you working with a translator? Pace it slow enough that they can work with you. Are there a lot of outside noises? Maybe you could invite the audience to come a little closer. Storytelling requires flexibility, so it works in a given context; it's your responsibility to respond to the situation.

When you know the context within which you are telling stories, you can make better choices, be more respectful, and have a more effective and enjoyable performance.

Continuing education

c

If you are passionate and dedicated to your profession, it's worth pursuing continuing education, no matter how much of a master you already are. Conferences, workshops, master's classes, and coaching are all ways to continue to hone your craft.

Conferences are a good place to start. Not only are there workshops on a wide range of topics, but you can also spend time talking with colleagues, so you can bat ideas around and help each other become better at what you do. I've often heard people bemoan limitations in conference workshop offerings, so I remind you that everyone has their own way of doing things. You may already consider yourself an expert at a facet of your work, but you can probably learn more by listening to how other people do it.

When I attend a workshop, even if it's about a topic I know, I am exposed to another way of thinking. By going through the exercises and participating, I learn from others in the class, be they masters or novices. When I go to conferences, I often try to attend workshops for beginners because it never hurts to go back to basics. I learn something every single time.

Talking with my colleagues means I am exposed to more ideas and approaches than I ever would be if I were I to isolate myself. It helps me when someone I respect challenges my ideas and makes me work through my reasoning. The conference means I will have several conversations, maybe aided by a martini or two, where I will get fired up and remember that part of what I love about this work is the intellect.

Maybe conferences, workshops, or master classes are too expensive or too far away for you. Host an experienced storyteller and offer them a chance to run a workshop from your home. This helps your local storytelling community and gives you a chance to learn from a master, up close and personal.

If that seems like too much work, consider coaching. Many coaches work through online live-video services (or other distance learning solutions) so you don't even need to be near someone to work with them. Most of my coaching clients are long-distance.

You may also want to develop a formal mentoring relationship with a storyteller you admire. They are not obligated to mentor you, so if you approach someone, do so respectfully and be willing to take no for an answer, but if you find a mentor who is good for you, it can be a very fruitful experience.

If all these feel daunting, consider going to a local performance, watching videos of other storytellers, reading a book of folktales and adapting one, writing a list of 10 things you'd like to learn, or something else just to give yourself the option to grow and learn more about your work.

Continuing education opportunities are everywhere. Reading, talking, going to events, observing the world and more. Every time we consider our art and take a risk, we are learning. When we learn, we grow and become better tellers and more engaged listeners.

Contracts

I know, this seems like the boring part of being a storyteller, but it is a mark of professionalism and helps both you and your client set clear expectations. You may want to call it a Performance Agreement if that feels a little easier but use one for every single gig. You and the person hiring you should sign and date it, and you should have a copy at hand if there are any questions. A verbal agreement is worth the paper it's not printed on.

Your contract should include:

◆ Your name and contact information, including cell phone number and email.
◆ Your client's name and contact information, including cell phone number.
◆ Type of program with a short description (1–2 sentences). Some people also include the formal description of the program that will be consistent in all marketing materials.
◆ Date of the program.
◆ Exact time.
◆ Exact location.
◆ Expected audience, type, and size.
◆ Performance room setup including amplification or other technology needs.
◆ Exact fees you will charge and for what, including travel expenses, meals, housing, etc.
◆ If you have discounted your fee, list your regular fee then the discount, so your client (and anyone they know) knows the value of what they are getting.
◆ Payment expectations, including who will pay you, when, what percentage is to be paid in advance or after, how long they can take to pay you, etc.
◆ Cancellation policy, specifying a number of days in advance and money to be paid even if the performance is canceled if notice is not given in time. You may also want to include provisions for running late, inclement weather, and that you will still be paid even if the audience is not what's expected.
◆ Set out the procedure for a "change of plans" for both parties, including dates, times and locations.
◆ Specify that all recording and photography must be done with teller's permission.
◆ Clarify if the sale of books and tapes is permitted and if the host client gets a percentage. (Find how much others sell so you can gauge how much material to take with you.)
◆ Clarify if your client wants these materials ahead of time or if you can bring them yourself to the performance.

◆ Inquire who is expected to book the airline, hotel, provide meals and if you will be given any petty cash for expenses.
◆ Request copies of all publicity and promotion generated by your client.
◆ If your show includes challenging material (cursing or content) you may want to include a free speech clause that ensures this is understood by the hiring party and permitted.

This may sound like a lot, but it really is standard stuff and protects everyone involved. Search the internet for "sample performer contract" to get a template you may then customize.

Current events and news

C

We are surrounded by a steady stream of current events coverage, making it very hard to escape the challenging events that seem to occur daily in this world we live in. As storytellers, we can talk about news events in a variety of ways.

We can **tell personal stories** about our reaction to the news. This could include recollections, stories about people we know or have created who were present during an event, or other realistic stories. These stories help us all remember we're not alone in our reactions to these difficult times and can bring new information to your listeners. The danger is that the storyteller must be able to tell the tale without falling apart. You don't want your audience to have to take care of you, instead of being immersed in their own response to the story.

We can **tell allegories**. Many traditional stories can easily be recast into responses to current events. This lets us think about the tough stuff through metaphor. Just make sure your audience has room to come to the metaphor on their own terms. Equally, understand what your story is about. In 2013 I retold *The Abduction of Persephone* from her mother's point of view. This was a week or two after the shootings in Newtown, CT. It was only midway through the story I realized that I was telling a story of parental grief, so we could all grieve these lost children. It was a hard moment in the telling when I had to rely on professionalism to keep going.

We can **acknowledge the event and move on**. Sometimes we just need to move past something and proceed as we originally intended. If the event is big enough, it becomes another presence in the room. Acknowledging it means your listeners know that you understand why they might be distracted. They know you are, too. And they know that together perhaps you can escape for just a little while.

We can **use the event to create a new story**. How many of us have stories about where we were when we heard about 9/11? The Challenger explosion? The King and Kennedy assassinations? What about a story of foreclosure or marching for civil rights or watching the moon landing? We can take those moments after they've had time to crust over, put them in a personal and historical context, and build something new. We can share our lives and our history with each other, using those moments to talk about something else entirely.

We also must remain aware of the context within which we tell our stories. Current events may lead us to select or exclude stories for a given event.

Every storyteller must contend with the world beyond their performance. We are lucky, our work is about connecting with other human beings. When we remember we are of the world, not separate from it, even the most difficult moment can be wrapped in a story.

Cursing and other ways of transgressing boundaries

c

Language conveys meaning. Some storytellers use harsher language than others or enjoy being a little more shocking, and we must decide what kinds of boundaries we are willing to transgress. Each time you tell a story you make choices about the aesthetics you present.

Some of this is generational and cultural. These kinds of issues have been around since there were generations and are present in every aspect of human life. I imagine Australo-pithecus parents shaking their heads at the outrageous antics of their young.

I find value in telling stories that deal with difficult or challenging material, but I make sure it's appropriate to the audience. I check with the curator and I make my own decision in the moment (for example, there may be children in an audience I was told would be only adults). Kids in the audience may change my content though I have been known to talk with parents when they bring children to a show advertised as adults-only. Every venue I have ever run has a free-speech clause, asking only that tellers let the audience know if they are including PG-13 or greater content so the audience can decide if they want to hear it. If you are including transgressive material in your shows, make sure the organiz-ers know and consider including a free speech clause in the contract.

Even as someone who finds value in transgressive storytelling, I still want to behave pro-fessionally, so I take other factors into consideration.

- ◆ **Use common sense.** If you are hired to tell to preschoolers, tell stories that don't include swear words. Give parents forewarning if they show up at an adult-oriented gig with their kids. If you're telling to 90-year-old nuns, you may need to mind your manners. Common sense goes a long way.
- ◆ **Authenticity matters.** If the language makes sense in the context of the story and who you are, then it belongs there. I would never, ever ask a teller to be anything but authentic.
- ◆ **Let the audience self-censor.** I make sure my curator and my audience know what they are in for. I believe in free speech. I also believe that everyone can choose what they are exposed to. Let your audience know you use salty language so they can decide if they want to hear it or not.

◆ **Diversity and representation matter.** This includes having a wide range of stories available for audiences. Some tellers who are uncomfortable with transgression have audiences who adore them because those are the stories they need. So too will the tellers who push boundaries

◆ **Ultimately, you need to decide what is most appropriate for your story, your audience, and yourself.** Be aware that there may be consequences to your choices and know that you are being deliberate in what you choose to say on stage.

A place for your thoughts.

Death

This is not an exploration of the morbid or maudlin, but a look at how storytellers handle death in their stories.

Death is part of life; it's one of our very few certainties. It's also something few of us speak about easily since it's emotionally fraught. As storytellers, we have a precious opportunity to help our audiences think about loss, one of the more difficult things we experience, in a safe environment, through the powerful medium of story.

Traditional material is rich with stories about death: King Arthur, Isis and Osiris, Gelert, Red Riding Hood (read older versions), The Three Little Pigs, Pandora's Box. These stories have helped us to understand why we must die and some of the actions that can lead to our deaths. They show us the culturally defined differences between a good death and a bad death, never letting us forget that eventually, we all die, as will the people we love.

Modern life is full of stories about death, too. Open any news site, read any newspaper, look at Facebook any day and you'll find a story about someone who died, how they lived their life and how they want to be remembered.

Telling these stories helps our audiences remember that death is part of human experience and there are tools we can use as we grieve. They can also help us with our own struggles with death.

For example, when I was 26, I had cancer. I faced the very real possibility of my own death and had to help those around me find a way to process the idea of my loss. I found solace and comfort in the story of Gilgamesh, the ancient Sumerian myth in which Gilgamesh the king tries and fails to bring his best friend back from the dead. Eventually, I turned this most ancient of stories into a performance, bracketing the myth with a personal context. Telling it helped me heal and overcome the fear of my own death. It also helped those around me remember that we all die. I didn't tell it publicly until I was sure I could do so in a way that was safe for me and the audience. Twenty years later (almost to the day), my husband died of pancreatic cancer. I have crafted several stories about love and death since; they have helped me process his loss and they have helped members of the audience process their own losses.

D

As storytellers, we must be sure that we can get out of the audience's way so they can do their own work as they listen. If we become too emotional, beyond the appropriate boundaries of the performance, it will jolt the audience from their own imagination and instead focus their attention on us and our needs. If we tell a story about death, we must be sure we are doing so in service to the story, the audience and the world, in addition to whatever personal drive we may have to tell it.

We need these stories because they move us to feel and then to act. They guide us through our own grief, reminding us that we are not alone. They show us paths to live the kinds of lives that will be remembered and sometimes, are examples of the way death matters. They are roadmaps not to death, but to life.

Dialogue

Well done dialogue in performance storytelling is all but invisible. The audience knows it's happening, understands it, and is not sidetracked by it. When it's poorly done, dialogue becomes confusing and distracting.

Here are some tips to using dialogue well when telling a story:

- **Is the dialogue essential?** Do the characters really need to talk it through in front of the audience or can you tell us the outcome of the conversation?
- **Can you use your body to differentiate the speakers?** Simply shifting your weight from one side to another may be enough to differentiate between speakers. You can also use body language instead of words for portions of the dialogue. Instead of saying, "I don't know" could the character shrug instead?
- **Keep it short.** The dialogue shouldn't be very long in solo performance storytelling. Instead you can convey dialogue by talking about reactions or outcomes.
- **Be careful with voices.** Make sure your character voices (if you have them) are consistent.
- **Observe how other storytellers handle dialogue.** What do you find effective? What isn't?

When you manage your dialogue well and use it only when essential, your stories will deepen and your audiences will come along for the ride.

Difficult stories

Why do some storytellers talk about loss or trauma? Why do audiences listen to them? We need difficult stories because we need to know we are not alone. A well-told difficult story with good structure and resolution will help your audience know that they are not the only ones who have been to hell and survived.

We build community by sharing our stories of adversity and survival. If you are drawn to telling difficult stories, don't treat the audience as if they are your therapist. Remember that they are looking to you for guidance through the darkness. You become their light by telling the difficult story with craft, precision, authenticity, some vulnerability, and truth.

Some difficult stories take more honing and craft than others, so you can keep your audience safe. Talk them through with your friends and colleagues, but don't be afraid to tell them.

One of my signature stories deals with suicidal behavior and feelings. It's a metaphorical story about a very dark time in my life, one I survived. There was a time when I didn't like to tell it because I thought no one would want to hear it, but I paid attention to the reactions of my audience. Almost every time I told it, someone afterward would come up to me and thank me, saying they never knew anyone else felt that way. They would tell me they felt less alone and maybe now could go get help. I came to realize that for every person who spoke with me, I didn't know how many didn't choose to, but maybe felt a little less alone.

Tell your difficult stories to appropriate audiences. Tell them well and with authenticity. You never know whose life you may save.

Endings

Endings matter. A poorly executed ending can ruin an otherwise beautifully told story, while a fantastic ending can support a story that was wobbling. The ending need not be a clear resolution nor is every ending happily ever after, but it does need to leave the audience with a sense of completion or at least satisfaction and curiosity.

The crucial elements for effective endings are:

◆ **You like the ending.** It gives you a sense of completion and you feel as though the story is at a natural resting place.
◆ **The audience is left with a sense of completion.** They may have questions, they may be uncomfortable, but they leave the story experience knowing this was a stopping point.
◆ **The audience is not left worried about you.** If you're telling a personal story, they must be able to walk out of the experience believing you will be okay. It's cruel to do otherwise and doesn't let the audience have their own relationship with the story, per the story triangle. It also turns the storytelling experience from art and performance to therapy.
◆ **The ending is related to the rest of the piece.** An ending completely disconnected may be interesting art, but it doesn't serve the audience's narrative expectation.
◆ **Ideally, the ending is memorable.** It might be zinger or a particularly touching moment, but no matter how you craft it, you want your audience to remember it.

Give your listeners a cue that you're done. Bow. Pause and smile. Say thank you. This is especially useful when you aren't using a formulaic ending like "happily ever after."

Some stories don't have well-defined endings, because not everything in life comes to an easy resolution, but you can acknowledge that in a variety of ways. For example, because storytelling can easily violate the fourth wall, the teller can directly address the audience.

◆ Jack and the princess stood there, looking at each other. I don't know how this story ends, but I do know this: The giant was dead. The princess was free. Jack discovered himself to be a rich man, and that, of course, is another story.
◆ We are still growing and changing. I don't know what the future will bring, but I know we'll face it together.
◆ And I am still here.

A good ending, one with an emotional and narrative punch, can elevate an otherwise adequate story. Your audience may remember your ending long after the other memories fade; don't neglect it. Give it the time and attention it deserves, both you and your audiences will be happier and more satisfied for it.

Ethics

Storytelling is a powerful tool. We are hardwired to respond to narrative; it's one of the most direct ways to trigger emotion which triggers action. As a result, there are a wide range of ethical issues we must take into consideration.

These include:

◆ What kind of influence do I want to have on my audience?
◆ How do I want them to feel? What do I want them to remember?
◆ What material do I tell, what boundaries do I enforce?
◆ How can I build up my coaching clients without giving them false hope?
◆ When I teach, how do I encourage my students to use storytelling to create meaningful change, to be entertaining and empowering, and to not use its power for ill?
◆ As an organizational storyteller, what organizations do I want to empower to use story more effectively? Do they align with my ethics?

Sometimes the ethical choices are obvious. For example, shortly after the Gulf oil spill, I was contacted by an organization involved in the accident. They wanted help telling the story of the spill so they wouldn't appear to be culpable but could be the heroes instead. They knew that for good spin they needed a good story. I was recommended to them by someone at another organization with whom I had worked. I did not find the organization nor what they were asking me to do to be ethical. I was polite and firm. I thanked them for their interest and turned them down.

This job would have netted me more income than any other job I have ever had. They could afford it. They were desperate. But I couldn't work with one of the organizations I felt was to blame for an environmental disaster.

Because my work is so integral to who I am, it's important for me to work with people and organizations I am not repulsed by. When I'm lucky, they are people and causes I actively support. It's important to charge the appropriate fee, so I remind the people hiring me that arts are valuable. I have guidelines around appropriation, around what kinds of stories I tell to whom, about how I teach, and so on.

Other choices are less clearly ethical issues, but they have ethical considerations. Should you charge less to get more work? What about telling a personal story in which someone still living behaved badly? How bound to the facts do you need to be in true stories? I could go on and on, but you get the point.

Every teller must understand their own ethics. They must consider what they will and won't do, who they will and won't work with, what *truth* means to them, how they will ethically teach, etc. These seem like big issues, but most storytellers already have a sense of this, because they make choices based on their ethics every single day. Storytelling is such a powerful tool; each teller must decide how they will use that power.

E

Event planning

E

It is likely you will need to plan events in your storytelling career. As performers, we sometimes must make our own venues, so it's a good idea to have a sense of the tasks involved before you start.

Whether your event is a house concert, an ongoing venue, or a festival you must do several things to prepare. There are many comprehensive guides to event planning, but here are some basic things to consider as you negotiate your contract and after.

- ◆ **Venue.** Is your venue appropriate to the event and budget?
  - ❖ Have they hosted storytelling before? Do they appreciate your craft?
  - ❖ Are the stage and technical aspects appropriate for your needs? Do they provide technical support including amplification, setting out chairs, and other logistics?
  - ❖ Is the owner of the venue willing and able to help you with some of the marketing, like putting the event up on their webpage?
  - ❖ What do they expect you to do for them?
- ◆ **Ticketing.** Is ticketing necessary and how will the money be managed?
  - ❖ If you're selling advanced tickets, you want to do ticketing through a service like Brown Paper Tickets or Eventbrite?
  - ❖ Who collects the money?
- ◆ **Audience.** Whom do you want to attract and how will you attract them?
  - ❖ How do you reach them to let them know about this event?
  - ❖ What stories will they want to hear?
- ◆ **Performers.** Are you hiring other performers to work with you?
  - ❖ Have a contract or other document that states what you expect of them and what they can expect from you.
  - ❖ Confirm with them a few weeks before the event.
  - ❖ Ask them to promote the event.
- ◆ **Marketing.** How do you plan to get people in the door?
  - ❖ Where will you run ads and what is your budget?
  - ❖ Who will help you with this?
  - ❖ Do you have a press list or connections with others who might get the word out?
- ◆ **Food/drink.** Should food and drink be available?
  - ❖ If the venue is providing food/beverages, do they have the appropriate licensing? Is everything labeled for allergies?
  - ❖ If you are providing food is everything appropriately labeled? Do you need to worry about local victualing ordinances?

- ❖ If you are providing alcohol, do you have the right liability insurance? Would it be worth hiring a bartender?
- ◆ **Programming.**
  - ❖ Know what you will do ahead of time. Whether that means you have a specific program planned or a range of stories to pick from, know your material.
  - ❖ Likewise, if you have other performers, make sure everyone knows the performance order.
  - ❖ You also must ensure that the performance meets marketing expectations and that most of your audience will be satisfied.
- ◆ **Programs and sale items.** You want your audience to go home with a piece of you or at least with a chance of remembering you.
  - ❖ If you provide a program, make sure it includes your contact information.
  - ❖ Set up a place where they can sign up for your mailing list.
  - ❖ If you are selling items, please make sure your money collection system works before the event.

A place for your thoughts.

Fairy and folktales

When you hear "fairy and folktale" do you automatically think of a sweet story for children? Do you assume all folktales are simple? If so, you're cutting yourself off from one of the most powerful forms of story. These tales from the oral tradition are from every culture and cover most aspects of human experience. As a storyteller, it's worth working with them. They'll help you expand your imagination, connect with the past and understand how symbols can work in a story. Your audiences will also find comfort in the rhythms of a fairy or folktale, so it's a good idea to have a few handy.

Fairy and folktales are different. Fairy tales have some kind of magical element, while folktales may not. Fairy tales may also be literary stories, though I encourage you to stick with those in the public domain, while folktales are always from the oral tradition. A quick internet search will help you learn more about the similarities and differences.

These stories capture the whole range of human experience in symbolic language: Growing up, leaving home, conquering fears, being disregarded or overlooked, growing old and dying. They help us understand ourselves and how our individual experiences are more alike than different. They give us a roadmap to use as we travel our lives. They are the stories that ripple through our cultures and our lives, giving us a common language with which to understand the world.

Here are some points to consider when you work with fairy and folktales.

◆ **Just because it's a fairy or folktale doesn't mean it's a simple story.** Many stories are dark, frightening, or at a minimum explore some of the more challenging times of life (childlessness, parental abandonment, learning who you are, adolescence, etc.). So, spend some time with the story and decide how you want to tell it and the key elements.

◆ **Understand where the story comes from.** These stories come with a cultural context, so you should have some understanding of where the story comes from and what it means in context. If there are words you don't know, find out. If there's something that doesn't make sense to a modern audience, consider changing it to something that does (e.g. if a character is wearing a "girdle" in the text, perhaps you should say "belt").

◆ **Explore why the story appeals to *you*.** Fairy and folktales are rife with symbols, so it's worth spending some time understanding why a story appeals to you, what the symbols mean to you. This can be the work of years, so please tell the story as you unfold it, but just don't be surprised if it has unexpected meaning for you.

- **If you change the story do so carefully, without stripping the heart out of the story.** The Disney version of The Little Mermaid overlooks her death at the end, entirely changing the meaning of the story. If you change a story, understand why you're doing it and how the meaning will be altered. If you modernize the story, honor the original text in whatever way makes the most sense to you; please consider carefully before you take all the tough stuff out of a story. It's probably there for a reason – the reward at the end may be more meaningful if the journey was arduous.

- **Consider the viewpoint you want to use while telling the story.** Do you want to focus on the happy endings or the dark journey? Are you more interested in the voice of a minor character? What about the villains?

- **Select the right story for the audience.** This is a tenet no matter what kind of story you're telling. Be wary of using accents unless you're very good at them, and if you tell stories *from* a particular culture *to* that culture and you're not *of* that culture, treat the stories with utmost respect. Be prepared to get some challenging feedback from people of the culture. For example, I have told Irish fairy tales and been told by people with Irish grandmothers that my telling is very different, and implied inadequate, compared to what they grew up with. This doesn't mean I don't tell these stories; I just try to tell them respectfully and understand that my telling cannot equal a telling in a deep cultural context.

Fairy and folktales are among the most enjoyable stories you can tell; they are deep in our psyches and convey experiences we can all relate to. Who hasn't been lost in the woods or undertaken a journey from home? Enjoy telling these stories. They are part of our human heritage. Just don't forget to do the same work you would for any other kind of story.

Fourth wall

Wikipedia defines the fourth wall as, "...a performance convention in which an invisible, imagined wall separates actors from the audience. While the audience can see through this 'wall', the convention assumes, the actors act as if they cannot." You've undoubtedly experienced this. The actors in a play go about their business as if the audience is not there, as if they aren't being watched.

Storytelling is much more flexible. You can, if you choose to, interact with the audience more directly and include them in the immediate moment of the story. I love doing this and find audiences enjoy it, too.

- **Interactive stories** give the audience a place to participate as a group. For example, in one story, the audience makes various animal noises when I cue them. In another story, I encourage the audience to beat out a rhythm with their feet.
- You can **bring an audience member on stage** for certain kinds of participatory stories, inviting them to become part of the scenery or to embody a character. Thank them and give them a round of applause.
- **Invite the audience to give you story elements.** For example, you could say, "Once upon a time there was a little.... A little what?" then run with their suggestion.
- My favorite way of breaking the fourth wall lies in **asides and secrets**. I have several stories where I move into the audience and chat directly with audience members about what's happening in the story at that moment. In others, I may whisper something in someone's ear if it's appropriate to the story.

The lack of the fourth wall means you can interact with your audience and make them even more a part of the storytelling moment. While it can be a little risky, it is far more likely to lead to fun story adventures and the audience feeling as if they were part of something special.

Fracturing stories

Many people love fracturing fairy tales. It gives the teller a chance to recast a story in ways that may be more appropriate for their own lives, their audience, and their environment. When you fracture a story, you will alter elements, so it becomes something new, yet it is still recognizable by the audience. Even if you aren't interested in changing traditional material, playing with how a story is told is always a good exercise.

F

Before we start, I want to stress that you should know your original story well before you break it apart. Tell a standard version several times so you solidly understand the plot, structure, why the story matters to you, and how it works with an audience.

To understand how to fracture a story you much first understand how a story works, what it is composed of.

Every told story comprises six elements:

◆ Character and point of view
◆ Setting
◆ Voice
◆ Plot and conflict
◆ Context
◆ Structure

Of these, you can tinker with four elements when fracturing a known story:

◆ Character and viewpoint
◆ Setting
◆ Voice
◆ Structure

If you want the story to remain familiar to the audience, you can't change the basic plot too much or they won't recognize it easily, nor does any teller have detailed control over who is in their audience and what context they are telling the story into.

Character and viewpoint
By changing your protagonist, you change the tale. What if you told Little Red Riding Hood from the wolf's viewpoint? Or the grandmother's? You can also explore unexpected points of view. For example, what if you told the same story as a news report on

local television? Or from the viewpoint of the grandmother's house, now abandoned in the woods? What if you changed the gender of the main character or the villain? How would that impact the story?

Changing viewpoint allows you to create empathy where none may have existed before, and to use your stories to make other points.

Setting
Most fairy tales are set in a "once upon a time." We each have our own images of that time and place, but generally, it's somewhat rustic or quaint, old-fashioned, and white.

What if you change the time of the story? Set Beauty and the Beast in Neolithic times or in your own neighborhood now? Who would the Beast be?

You could change the environment. Instead of a forest, imagine a city, a school, or a camp.

Voice
Changing a story from third to first person can be powerful. Let Cinderella tell her own tale. Maybe she enjoyed those quiet moments by the fire and was rather overwhelmed by all the attention at the ball. If you change both voice and protagonist, you may end up with a dramatic retelling. What if Cinderella's sister told the story in her old age, as she sits maimed and alone? How would she tell it?

Structure
Playing with structure is somewhat more complex. We can think of structure as a formula that makes building a story easier. Satisfying stories must have beginnings (A), middles (B) and ends (C). It can sometimes be hard to figure out each part, so if we think of the story structure as a formula, that may make it easier. Some common formulas are:

A-B-C
  Once there was this person/event/thing. These things happened. It ended this way.

A-B-A
  Now-then-now-conclusion/how things change
  Here-there-here-conclusion
  My story-your story-my story

C-A-B-C
  Begin with the end, then tell the events leading to it. A story that starts with a flashback might use a structure similar to this one.

A place for your thoughts.

Gratitude

We are so lucky to do this work. No matter the size of your audience, if we have one person who really wants to hear us, we're far luckier than many, many people. No matter what critique we receive, if we get up and tell again, we are lucky and strong and can be grateful for the opportunity. No matter if we fail, make a mistake, struggle with jealousy or insecurity or any of the other demons that haunt us, every time we stand on a stage, we are so lucky that we can step beyond our own limitations.

G

We are so lucky to hear these stories. Every time we listen to a story we are being shown into someone else's world in a deep and intimate way. Every time we listen deeply to a storyteller, we are giving them the gift of doing the work they love. Every time we are kind to a beginning storyteller or are moved by an accomplished one, we are opening ourselves up to awe, to connecting with someone else, to stopping the tumult for just a little while.

This is no accident. By our own hard work, talent and the whim of the universe, we can stand up and tell stories in front of interested audiences, be they kids, festival crowds, business people, or conference attendees. This is something to be grateful for. By cultivating a sense of gratitude for your work, your audiences, your colleagues, and more, you become more resilient when things aren't just right and more receptive to opportunity. Ongoing research has established that cultivating gratitude makes everything better.

◆ **Gratitude opens the door to more relationships.** Storytelling is all about relationships. When we are grateful for those relationships and express that gratitude, we are more likely to be remembered and invited back. When I let my audiences know I am grateful for their time, when I thank those who hire me, I am letting them know that they are just as valued as anyone else. We all need to hear that from time to time.

◆ **Gratitude improves physical health.** My body is my instrument. When I am grateful for it, I take better care of it. If gratitude will help my body endure all I put it through (this traveling life takes a toll) then I will be grateful for it every day!

◆ **Gratitude improves psychological health.** When we are grateful, we are less likely to hold onto toxic emotions. What I am feeling is reflected in my performance, no matter how practiced I am. If I take the stage with gratitude, I am less likely to remain annoyed at the promoter who misspelled my name or any of the other myriad annoyances.

- ◆ **Gratitude enhances empathy and reduces aggression.** Storytelling is all about building empathy. Our brains are more likely to respond empathetically when we hear a story. If gratitude will help me feel more empathy, then I'm all for it.
- ◆ **Grateful people sleep better.** Studies suggest writing in a gratitude journal before going to sleep can improve sleep. As storytellers, we need to be rejuvenated and sleep helps.
- ◆ **Gratitude improves self-esteem.** Who doesn't need a little help here now and again? We are more likely to stop comparing ourselves to others when we feel grateful for them.
- ◆ **Gratitude increases mental strength.** We all need strength. Performing can be exhausting.

We are so lucky. Remember that and be grateful. Be grateful for every performing opportunity, for every audience member, for every time you hear a story even if you've heard it a million times already. When we are grateful, we expand the possibilities for storytelling. Our gratitude will be obvious to the world.

Healing

The Cracked Pot, a story from India.

A water-bearer carries two large pots on a yoke across his shoulders up the hill from the river to his master's house each day. One has a crack and leaks half its water out each day before arriving at the house. The other pot is perfect and always full of water after the long walk from the river.

Finally, after years of arriving half-empty, the cracked pot apologized to the water-bearer. It was miserable. "I'm sorry that I couldn't accomplish what the perfect pot did."

The water-bearer says, "What do you have to apologize for?"

"After all this time, I still only deliver half my load of water. I make more work for you because of my flaw."

The man smiled and told the pot. "Do you see all the lovely flowers growing on the side of the path where I carried you? I noticed your leak and scattered seeds. The flowers are so bright because of the water you leaked. There are no flowers on the perfect pot's side."

None of us is without flaw, without pain, without scars and cracks.

When we tell our own stories of pain and survival, we heal. When we listen to others tell their stories, we heal. You don't have to be a therapist, you need only be an ordinary compassionate human being who listens to someone else. As tellers, we can process our own pain and turn it into performance that is, as Texas storyteller Elizabeth Ellis puts it, a roadmap to hell and back. *I went there, the same place you are now. I survived. I returned and I healed. Here is a map.*

Storytelling helps us heal.

I have seen miracles. There was the woman who began telling the story of her rape, over and over, and now sings praise songs to the universe. I know of a man who told the story of his son's birth and death so he and his family could heal. He discovered along the way that he was celebrating his son's life. My own retellings of fairy tales and myths that are really about mental illness or loss. Storytelling helps us heal.

This has been the case since we began to communicate. Think of Prometheus' terrible pain, of Ishtar's grief, on and on. Story can help us heal.

One necessary addendum to healing stories: It is important that you understand why you are telling a healing story and make sure you're telling it to the right audience. If you're telling a story about trauma in performance, you must ensure that a) the audience knows you are okay now, so they can have their own experience of the story without worrying about you and b) you don't traumatize them by telling the story without giving them a chance to opt out. You never know what an audience member may be experiencing. If your story is about sexual violence, a content warning is appropriate.

Storytelling can be healing for the teller and for the listener. We just must ensure we take care of each other along the way.

Historical tellings and voicing the unvoiced

I had the honor of presenting a commissioned work in celebration of Women's History Month on the life and influence of Sojourner Truth. It was a wonderful and challenging experience, well-received, that got me thinking about how storytellers can, should and sometimes should not give voice to the unvoiced.

To remind you, Sojourner Truth was of African descent, born into slavery in New York state in 1797. She was named Isabella Baumfree. She self-emancipated in her late 20s and began to preach on both salvation and emancipation. In her 40s, she renamed herself Sojourner Truth and added women's suffrage to her speeches. She was illiterate but with the help of a friend published her autobiography when she was 50. She continued to speak and preach on emancipation, equality and women's suffrage for the rest of her life. Truth died in her mid-80s, having seen the end of slavery across the nation but not the vote for women or anything resembling equality for black people.

Developing this piece presented some challenges. Among them:

◆ I was hired as a storyteller, so I knew I didn't need to present it as a lecture, but I was telling historical fact. I wanted to get all the data right so I faced a puzzle: How should I merge detailed historical data and immersive story?
◆ More importantly, how could I tell the story of an enslaved African-American woman who died over 130 years ago without straying into appropriation? I certainly wasn't going to put on blackface or pretend to speak in her voice. We don't know what she sounded like, her accent or even what she really said. Beyond that, it would be insulting were I to try to imitate her.
◆ How could I tell her story with any authenticity when she never wrote a thing down? Everyone who *did* write something down inevitably filtered it, because her story was written by middle-class, free, white people, all of whom had their own agenda. I have my own agenda but mostly I want her to be heard and not forgotten.
◆ Finally, I wanted to be giving my client what they needed. How to do that?

These were not the only challenges I faced when putting this together, but they were the most compelling. What follows are some thoughts and the solutions I enacted.

Giving voice to the voiceless.

As a storyteller, part of my job is to give voice to the voiceless. I love telling fairy-tales from unexpected points of view, so the overlooked characters have a chance to speak. I enjoy playing devil's advocate and giving the villain voice. I view it all as a part of my work in the world, allowing my listeners a chance to consider another viewpoint. Storytellers can be especially subversive with this aspect of our work since oral storytelling is such an effective way to build empathy. This is part of why I was so excited about this piece. I knew this was an unparalleled chance to talk about issues we still confront and to help ensure that someone amazing is not forgotten.

Data and narrative.

I am a storyteller. I am hired to help people connect emotionally with each other, with themselves and with a narrative. While I need to avoid factual errors, I need not turn the story into a recitation of dates and data points. By humanizing the data and events, I make it more relatable and, frankly, easier to tell. I can tell it as human experiences, not newspaper articles.

Working with my client.

This was the easiest of problems to solve. I made sure we each understood what we were getting and why. I asked about their goals and hopes for the piece. I listened. I did the best I could and tried to give them more than they were asking for, as I do with all my clients.

Authentic voice and appropriation.

Sometimes storytellers, in pursuit of authenticity, try to give literal voice to the unvoiced. They use accents or other tools to bring someone to life. I do not do that. If I can't do an accent perfectly, then it's insulting when I try. How often has a white person played a Native American in a film and used a generic "Indian" voice?

I needed to decide how I could tell this story with authenticity without being offensive.

For one, I am a short, white, middle-class, 21st-century woman who has always had the right to vote, not a tall, African-American woman, born into slavery in the 19th century who was arrested when she tried to vote. I could not be her on stage. It would be arrogant and inappropriate for me to try.

For another, we don't know what she sounded like. We know her first language was Low Dutch and that she learned English in her early teens. Most people who wrote down her words added Southern U.S. phrasing and cadence to them because by the mid-19th-century slavery was considered more of a Southern phenomenon even though people were enslaved in the North into at least the 1820s. In her lifetime, Sojourner Truth's actual voice was altered by her reporters to serve their own purposes. Truth knew of this and of the power it conveyed, so she didn't object as far as we know, but we don't know for sure.

If I'm not going to speak in her voice AND I want to build empathy and connection with my audience, avoiding giving a lecture, what could I do? I solved the problem with a variety of methods.

◆ I acknowledged this issue at the outset of the story.
◆ I used rich imagery to bring the audience back to her time, so they felt present in another place.
◆ I created a fictional amalgam who spoke in the first person. This white, middle-class woman knew Truth when she was young. She spoke to her experience with Truth. Yes, it could be argued that I am not a 19th-century woman and I did not know Truth, so how can I speak in her voice? I was willing to go this far. It is a personal choice and one I felt I could do with authenticity, integrity and without insulting Truth or the experience of the enslaved and unvoiced.
◆ At the end of the performance I reminded the audience we don't know how Truth sounded like as she spoke, but that she was a woman of great savvy. She had likely heard many pieces written about her and those written theoretically in her voice, so I concluded with a reading of her best-known speech. I did not try to sound like an aging African-American woman, nor did I try to change the language as it was written. I presented it as the closest approximation of her voice that we have, and I wanted her to have the last word.

None of these were easy choices to make and I'm certain I will keep modifying the program, but it was a fantastic experience, one that made me work and think hard, and question some of my beliefs about how professional storytellers present historical and underrepresented narrative.

These are all issues you will need to consider should you perform stories intended to give voice to the voiceless or do historical tellings.

Humor

Humor is an important part of storytelling. It can help underscore a point, ease a tense moment or just give the audience some fun. Think about how many humorous stories you've heard that still get a point across or how many speeches you've heard that use a joke to point out something that needs to be changed. Think about how often amid something deadly serious, we use a joke to take a breath. Think about how good it just feels to laugh.

H

Humorous stories differ from jokes. A humorous story intends to make the audience laugh but has a clear beginning, middle, end and an emotional arc. A joke is often more of an anecdote than a story. It can be part of a story but may not be the whole thing.

Regardless of whether you are telling a humorous story or a joke, please choose material appropriate to your audience, work on your timing and make sure you think it's funny. Give your audience time to laugh, don't rush them through the funny moment. If they don't laugh it doesn't mean they aren't amused, so be prepared for a variety of responses.

And remember, the best way to get to Carnegie Hall?
Practice.

Ideas, images, and storyseeds

Every storyteller and writer I know has been asked, "Where do you get your ideas?" Sometimes I want to reply that I belong to an idea delivery service and I get a fresh pack of ideas once a month, but that isn't helpful or even very funny.

The truth is that ideas for stories are everywhere. Observe the world you live in, and you will find seeds for the next story.

Ideas for stories can be found in our own lives, in the lives around us, in the news, in fiction, in nature and more. Once you have the start of an idea, play with the images. Let the image sit in you for a while, ideally when you have some time to let it grow. See what it suggests to you, what kind of story it might turn into.

This can take a while. For years I had an image of a drop of blood turning into a ruby. Eventually, this image grew into the story I call *Blood Woman* about a woman whose blood turns into rubies and her tears into diamonds. It's a big, long, complex story, and I'm glad I waited for the images to come clear.

I also regularly work with storyseeds, little ideas or questions that might lead to a story.

Storyseeds are all around. Ask yourself questions about why the world is as it is. Pick one thing and wonder about it. Maybe your next-door neighbor has a secret. Maybe they are really a minotaur and that explains why they always wear long pants. Maybe they used to be a prima ballerina. Maybe they are looking at you and wondering who you really are.

Stories are everywhere. Open yourself to them and they will come running.

Imagery and imagination

My favorite toy in the world is my imagination. As a storyteller, I get to play with my imagination and the imaginations of my listeners every day. It delights me and I hope it delights you.

Imagination is essential for any storytelling experience. Every time I work on a story, I draw on my imagination for images across the range of my sensory experience, so I can more fully paint the work I share with my listeners.

There is a world of difference between
Once upon there was an old woman who lived in a house
and
Once upon a time, there was an old woman with a red, floury apron and a three-legged dog. They lived together in a crooked house.

Or
When I was in fifth grade, I got picked on
and
When I was in fifth grade, I got used to the teasing about my ratty clothing. It was when they said I smelled that I felt my eyes sting.

The additional detail in both examples comes from imagining the scene with more clarity and deciding which images I want to share with my audience.

You must have clear images in your own mind to convey them to your audience. As you develop your story, ask yourself questions like:

◆ What color clothing did the main characters wear? Did they chafe? Were they new or old?
◆ How did the environment smell?
◆ Was it warm or cold? Raining? Clear?
◆ What did the inside of the porridge bowl look like? Was Red's cloak lined with satin? What color were Granny's eyes?

Imagination is like any other skill. You must practice to keep it agile and robust. Children have wonderful imaginations because they haven't yet bought the lie that they need to color within the lines. I urge you to stretch your imagination every single day. Your world will become more interesting and amusing if you do so. I love stretching my imagination with games like these:

◆ Next time you're on public transit or at a restaurant, look only at people's feet. Pick one pair of shoes and make up two stories about the wearer, one you think might be right and one you think is outrageously wrong. Then look at the rest of the person and decide which might be closer to the truth.

◆ Next time you're in slow traffic imagine you're in a very, very slow road race. Become the announcer.

◆ Go into a room you visit every day. Lie down on the floor and study the ceiling, something you likely ignore. Forget about the cobwebs – what other kinds of rooms could that ceiling belong to?

◆ Get some construction paper and crayons. Draw out the images from your stories. Map out the journey. See where you might go.

◆ Buy a coloring book and pull out your crayons again. Spend a little while with purple zebras, drawing in the background on the pages, going outside the lines.

When we deeply imagine something, when we populate it thoroughly with images across our senses and experiences, we make it live. We become better storytellers because the audience knows we believe what we're saying, that we have seen it, smelled it, tasted, heard and touched it. They imagine with us and we move into new worlds together.

Impossible

"What we need is more people who specialize in the impossible."

– Theodore Roethke

This is what storytellers do every day. We reinforce the idea that the impossible isn't so far-fetched after all. Whether we tell fairy tales and myths, redolent with wonder and magic, or personal stories of loss and triumph, we demonstrate repeatedly that human experience is universal and that we can connect with one another regardless of whatever boundaries seem to exist.

I specialize in the impossible. So do you.

◆ When I create a new story, I put together words and ideas in new ways. Sure, every story has already been told, but not the way I tell it. And not the way you would tell it. Storytelling is a continuous act of creation and recreation.
◆ When I tell stories, I create a world. What I say is then a vessel, taking you into your own imagination, hopes, dreams, fears, and adventures. I am not telling one story but a myriad of stories, one for each listener, all in one voice.
◆ When I listen to your story, sound waves travel through the very air and impact my tympanic membrane. I can make sense of those vibrations and turn them into meaning.
◆ What's more, listening to a story creates an alignment in neural activity that is the next best thing to telepathy. When we listen to each other, our brains look alike. We understand and experience more deeply than with any other form of communication.
◆ When I teach and coach, I help you find your own voice, your own understanding of your story; you have a chance to listen to yourself. In a world full of noise and distraction, it's nothing short of miraculous when we have a chance to listen to ourselves.
◆ My years of repeatedly telling stories of love and death have helped me remember that while I will never be the same after a loss or difficulty, I will survive. It is not impossible. Stories save lives. They have saved mine.

Embrace the impossible. Let it transform you.

Impostor syndrome

I regularly struggle with imposter syndrome and wonder if I have any right to do what I do, let alone try to help people. I ask myself questions like:

◆ Why would anyone want to hear my stories?
◆ I have nothing worthwhile to say, what makes me think I have any right to teach this stuff?
◆ How dare I send a newsletter to people who signed up for one? Isn't it an imposition?

I'm telling you this NOT so you will reassure me, but because I'm betting some of you question your own artistic worth occasionally, too. I know I can't stop you from doing this, but I remind you, your voice matters. The world needs our voices and talents. Please don't quit.

When my internal questioning becomes too loud and I struggle to work, if I'm lucky and smart, I do several things.

◆ **I get away from the work for a little while**, taking a little walk or do something else for a few minutes.
◆ **I might ask a friend** to tell me something to counteract the fear.
◆ **I do the work.** If I can make myself work for a while, the fear and disruptive thoughts will often go away.
◆ **I ask myself questions**, things like:
    ❖ Can you remember a single time your work seemed to make a difference for someone? (yes)
    ❖ Maybe you sometimes make it up as you go along. Does that make it less useful? (not usually) Doesn't that suggest that you know what you're doing since you *can* make it up? (yes)
    ❖ Why are you running yourself down like this? Is it about something else? (often) What can you do about that other thing?

You get the idea.

When we do something important and meaningful, sometimes old destructive patterns will crop up. Doing something meaningful can be frightening because the risks seem higher. They may be higher, but so are the rewards. The world needs your voice. Take a deep breath and keep telling.

Improvisation

Every storyteller should be able to do a little improvisation. In this context, *improvisation* refers to a theatrical technique, that ability to take a story and run with it, using ideas and suggestions from the audience. This is useful for many reasons.

◆ **It opens the door to new creativity and stories.**
If you play around with your stories by using improv techniques, you may learn something new about the story. You might learn something about a character or situation you never would have known had you stuck to the tried and true.

◆ **It helps you remain calm during interruptions or if you forget something.**
I've written about this elsewhere in this book, but if you are interrupted or forget something, improvising makes you more likely to weave the story back together with less distress.

◆ **It allows you to interact with the audience more.**
Because storytelling has no fourth wall, it can sometimes be fun to interact with the audience during a story. You might notice they particularly enjoy a description of a meal, for example. Improvising means you can spend a little more time in the meal with the audience.

◆ **It helps keep you flexible.** Being able to improvise will help you remain flexible in your performances and not become stuck to a single script.

◆ **It's fun.** It might not always be comfortable but playing around with improvisation is fun and will help you remain artistically nourished.

Consider taking an improv class or two at your local adult education center. You'll learn new skills, will meet interesting people and will add a new tool to your storytelling kit!

Intellectual property

I've been a performing storyteller for nearly 30 years. I have a very clear memory of the moment when I knew, without any doubt, this was the work I'd be doing for the rest of my life. It was a cold Tuesday night in Cambridge, Massachusetts. I was in a basement bookstore, Best Cellars Bookstore Cafe, at a storytelling event hosted by Brother Blue. I'd been attending these events for less than a year but I knew already this place was going to change who I was.

My story creation method then wasn't much different from the way it works now. I have an image I mull over and eventually a story builds around it, kind of the way a pearl begins from an oyster's irritation. I'd been playing with an image, a gathering of street people under a bridge. From there I added in the rain, the city and a period of my own occasional despair. A story. When it was my turn, I stood up and found myself telling what was to become Coyote On the Bridge, now one of my signature works. It deals with depression, suicidal behavior, the possible intervention by Coyote, the lost people of the city, and redemption. By the time I was done I was shaking and I knew this was my path, these kinds of meaningful stories that could change lives. I knew this story of my own dark times could save people. I knew what I had been born to do. Writing this down now it seems arrogant, but truly, it was one of those few moments when we know our entire purpose with utter clarity. To this day, every time I tell it someone comes up and says, "I never knew anyone else ever felt that way. Thank you." It was a defining moment.

I captured this story on my first recording, sold at various events and given to friends. I thought little of it because that's what storytellers do, we create and share our work.

Almost twenty years after I released that recording, I received an email from a man I didn't remember. He said we took a storytelling class together and there he bought my cassette. He was so moved by Coyote On the Bridge that he wrote a play based on it and was now in negotiations to see if it could be made into a film. He figured maybe he should get in touch and make sure, but I wouldn't mind, would I? He'd credit my story as the inspiration and that should be enough, right? He included a copy of the original play so I could see how important my inspiration was.

No. It wasn't okay. It wasn't enough and I did mind. My work had been stolen from me, certainly without malicious intent, but the play was such a close read of my story I felt violated. I expect I would have felt the same way had any of my stories been stolen, but this one had immense meaning and personal significance. I wrote back and told him

I could not give my approval. I explained why, both in personal terms and in legal terms. I also told him that if he continued, I would seek legal counsel. I rarely get angry and even less often on my own behalf, but I was furious.

As far as I know, he dropped the matter, but this incident clarified just how vulnerable storytellers are. There is a perception that because our work is spoken because it exists in the moment, it is more temporal and takes less effort to craft.

While the *performance* may be temporal, its effect is not. It took no less craft than a written story. There is no less personal investment in a told story than in any other kind of creative work. Yet because storytelling is a performance art, many storytellers and other artists seem to feel more comfortable using other's material without their permission.

It's not okay. Letting someone know after the fact isn't enough.

There are intellectual property issues you must consider when you tell traditional stories (can you craft a version unique to you, what sources are you using, etc.). This goes even further if you're interested in telling a story created by someone else. You must have their permission, preferably in writing, if you are going to tell someone else's story. It isn't honoring them to steal their work, even if you attribute it to them. If someone wants to tell one of your stories you have every right to say no, or yes, or let me think about it.

You may be thinking that stories don't belong to anyone and there are some that live in the public domain. Not all do, and they are not all ours to tell. Imagine you develop a story. You crafted it, honed the language and movements. You put your own experience and life into it. You discover that someone else is telling it as their own. How would you feel? I'd also add that I believe in as much open and accessible knowledge as possible. I just want artists to have ownership over their life and work.

My bottom line when considering what I want to tell is this: If I am not the creator of the work, do I have permission? How would I feel if someone stole my work (and I know, I felt awful)? What must I do so I can tell this ethically? And if I don't have permission to tell a piece someone else created, I take a deep breath and let it go. There are so many stories in the world. Why steal someone else's when I can create my own?

Interruptions

Every performer deals with interruptions sometimes; live performance is like that. I remind my students that it's their job to be prepared and have strategies to deal with noise, babies, puppies, trains, etc. They must be able to maintain their performance, their own comfort, and their connection with the audience.

Here are some tips that may help you, should you ever have to deal with interruptions to your show.

◆ **Prepare in advance.** Talk with the venue manager about what you might expect and what you can do ahead of time to minimize the likelihood of interruptions. Be prepared. That's the most important thing; stop problems before they start.

◆ **Know your material well.** If you do get interrupted, you want to be able to pick up where you left off without great difficulty. It will also make it easier for the audience to get back into the story.

◆ **As you go into the gig, think about how you might respond to a noise.** Will you incorporate it into the story? Will you wait until it stops? Will you acknowledge it happened, take a moment to chat with the audience, and then move on? What would be comfortable for you, so you have a plan?

◆ **Know your audience.** If you're telling at a family story hour, you might expect more interruptions than if you're telling in a black box theater. When you have some sense of what kinds of noise may happen you can strategize appropriately.

◆ **Remember that most of the time no one is making noise to sabotage you and acknowledging it may give everyone a chance to get over it.** People are people. Kids make noise. Trucks make funny sounds. Technical difficulties happen. By acknowledging that a noise has happened, demonstrating you're not upset about it and then moving on, you put your audience at greater ease.

I saw an excellent storyteller in performance with a kitten underfoot. She was telling a serious story, but the kitten kept wandering onto the stage, rubbing her legs and making adorable squeaks. Everyone was paying more attention to the cat than they were to the story. The storyteller looked down at the kitten, made the appropriate cooing noises, picked it up and held it while she continued her story. The audience could pay attention to her again because they weren't all thinking about how much they wanted to pet the kitty. The cat felt attended to and, when it wanted to jump down, it wandered away because it had received the attention it needed. She continued her story with the attention she deserved. It was masterful.

◆ **If your story is funny, give the audience time to laugh.** You may also experience unexpected audience laughter. Give them time to enjoy the moment.

◆ **If you must ask for help, do so politely so the audience remains on your side.** Give the noise maker another option. I was telling in a small tent at a festival with two young boys playing portable video games in the front row. The noise was distracting everyone. Their parents were nowhere in sight. I asked the boys if they could help me with my story. They were immediately engaged. I had them tell a couple of lines for me, then asked if they needed to keep playing their games, they might do so at the back of the tent. They didn't feel brushed aside and the audience could concentrate.

◆ **Remain flexible.** Life happens. You may need to change your performance a little or account for the unexpected. You can do that because storytelling is such a flexible and forgiving art form.

◆ **If you have a heckler, don't let it throw you.** Remember, the audience is likely on your side. Engaging with them will only make them fight back more.

Planning is the most important thing for dealing with an interruption. You should know what you will do should it happen as to avoid panicking when it inevitably happens. Planning helps you to make sure your audience feels cared for.

Isolation and community

We live in a culture that celebrates isolation. The myth of the artist in their lonely garret (and other cultural myths of lone heroes) has fostered a belief that the creative process thrives in isolation.

It doesn't.

Artists and most human beings are more effective and able to be their best when they have a community. Not that we don't need significant alone time to think, write, create, prepare, but we need time with those who share our passion and belief in our abilities to be the best artists we can be. We need allies.

Storytellers especially need to work in community, because the very nature of our work depends on other people. Our art may be practiced in isolation, but it comes to life when heard, in the moment.

You can find allies and community in many ways. Start going to storytelling open mics in your community. Find friends with whom you can bat around ideas. Talk with people in person or via video chat. Find online communities where your work is valued. Join professional organizations like The National Storytelling Network and go to conferences. Host a story salon where you listen and tell together. The possibilities are endless.

You can also ask an ally to listen to you and then just play around with story.

◆ **Freetell.** There is a writing technique called freewriting, where you write without stopping or regard for errors for a set amount of time, usually 5–15 minutes. When I freewrite I then circle the one phrase or word that seems most meaningful then free-write again using the word or phrase as my topic. After a round or two of freewriting, I often have something I really want to work on.

  In freetelling, I ask someone I trust to listen to me babble about the story for a set amount of time. That time is usually three minutes. When the time ends, I state what seemed most meaningful to me. I may ask the listener what struck them. I'll then tell the story with that information forefront in my mind.
◆ **Interview my characters.** Again, with a trusted listener I will assume the role of one of my characters. I will ask my listener to ask me questions and I will answer them as the character. How do I feel about the events in the story? What is my favorite ice cream? Who do I love, etc.? These questions give me new insight into the characters and the story. This is often enough to propel me out of a block.

◆ **Get appreciated.** Sometimes when I'm stuck, my internal demons shout: I'm not good at my art Who wants to hear meany way blah blah blah. When this happens, I find someone I respect who knows me and my work well. I ask them to tell me what they like about my work. I let them praise me. I remind myself that they are not lying. They are telling me about my own work from their perspective. I must hear them without filtering their comments through all the destructive thoughts I carry around. Once I've caught my breath, I get back to work and dive into the story again.

It may feel vulnerable, but when you have a community you trust to listen to and support you, when you have allies who you know believe in you, your work will grow, deepen, and be more effective when the time comes to shine.

Jealousy

I feel as though I should be writing this in a tiny font or some other way of indicating a secret, a shame. I know what I'm about to say does not differ from anything most of us feel, but we don't talk about it, and I think that can impact our work and our confidence in our abilities. It certainly undermines my sense of my own value as a storyteller, an artist, and a human being.

Here goes.

I love the villains in fairy tales. I know they can be truly awful and rarely do they actually learn a lesson – really, it's more about punishment – but they are so human. They are often the only characters who behave in understandable, if wicked, ways. They experience something that hurts. They lash out.

There are days when I am the Wicked Queen from Snow White. I look in my mirror and see myself as old, outdated. I am in that odd generational gap commonly known as Gen X, sandwiched between the Baby Boomers and Millennials. When I began storytelling, I was the baby in the room. When I tried to do new, innovative things (personal stories including sex, revamping fairy tales in experimental ways, creating judged storytelling events and so on) there was always someone telling me I was pushing too hard and no one would want that kind of stuff.

Now that kind of stuff is all the rage.

I often hear stories and see performances similar to what I was trying to do a decade or two ago. I celebrate that our art has grown so much and there is room for more diverse visions of what storytelling is. Even in my celebration, sometimes that hurt part of me thinks *what about me? I did that way back when and no one cared. I still do it. I still push boundaries. Does anyone care? I'm not the young generation now, does anyone want innovation from me?* I stifle those voices and carry on. They help no one. I'd rather keep doing new work and supporting other tellers, but those voices are there. While I don't lash out, I do get jealous.

There are days when I am the cursing fairy from Sleeping Beauty. I feel left out and so am less generous. I am the old woman in the road who offers spurned gifts. I am the giant who really just wants to be left alone. I am all of these villains some days.

What matters, of course, is what I do with these feelings. Most of the time I acknowledge them and move on. If it's a particularly bad day I might call a friend and rant for a while, then put on my big girl pants and try again. I do my best to not act on these feelings, to not become the wicked queen, even if I understand her more now than I ever thought I could when I was younger. To a large degree, it's the action (or lack thereof) that matters. All I can do is keep doing the best work I can and be as generous as I can be, regardless of some of my less noble feelings.

Who does jealousy hurt? If I don't act on it and do my best to remain a supportive member of the community, then I hurt no one, right? Isn't not acting on it enough? Wrong. I hurt myself because I doubt my own abilities, talent, and voice. I hurt others because, if I feel obsolete, I am less likely to seek out performances and teaching opportunities, so I remove my voice from the world. My voice matters, just as much as yours does, just as much as the newest storyteller who hasn't yet heard a broad range of performances so thinks all their ideas are new.

I know I'm not alone in this, but so rarely do I talk about it with anyone. A few colleagues have expressed similar feelings and I am grateful because I know I'm not the only one who feels petty jealousy sometimes. I know I'm not the only storyteller artist human being to feel this way. The old stories tell me that because there are so many characters who struggle with feeling left behind or worthless. The old stories don't offer a roadmap of a way out of these feelings. They tell me only that acting on them is evil. I remind myself that I still have worth even if I feel petty things. I do my best to not stifle others as I was stifled. I work to remain generous with my time, my mentorship, my leadership, my talent. But some days it's difficult and all I want is to have my mirror tell me that yes, I am still fair.

The storytelling community is amazing but still young, so we have no way to discuss these feelings in safe ways. We also live in a culture that doesn't support artists more generally, so there is little conversation about all the ways being an artist is also all the ways we are human, with good and bad feelings. I don't always know what to do with these emotions and I don't feel safe expressing them, but it is only by talking about them that we can remove the taboos and build a more inclusive storytelling world.

Karma

You know the basic concept, that what goes around comes around. This applies to storytelling as well. While I find some deep spiritual value in this, there are real, practical ways we can see karma at work in storytelling.

When storytellers practice *good listening*, when we remember that other tellers are as worthy of being heard as we are, we help build a community of listeners. And we need listeners for our own stories, so modeling good listening comes back to us. If we are ungenerous and don't listen to others, why should they listen to us?

When we are *ethical* about the gigs we take and refuse, passing on the ones we believe could be better fulfilled by other tellers, we help build a better reputation for storytelling as an art. None of us is accomplished at everything. When the right artist is in the right job we are viewed as more professional, more accomplished and more creative. We build a better environment for all of us to tell in. What's more, if we are generous and pass gigs to the right people, they are more likely to pass gigs back to us.

When we *help less experienced tellers* we are ensuring the art survives long after us. As we grow from new tellers to journeymen to mentors to elders, we can share our accumulated wisdom. Hoarding it won't help the world and won't help build a community of tellers and listeners.

These actions and more build good karma.

A story.

One of my signature stories is about a woman who is dissuaded from suicide by someone who might be Coyote. I've told this story hundreds of times. I know it makes an impression. I've been telling it for maybe 15 years.

Several years ago I received a thank you card from a suicide prevention organization, letting me know that a donation had been made in my honor. The note included an email address if I wanted to know more.

My curiosity couldn't be contained. I wrote and asked.

K

The donation was made by a mother. Her son had heard me tell my story, had talked to me after (she said he told me he didn't know anyone else ever felt that way. I've heard that a lot. Every time I tell people they aren't alone and they can get help if they need to). He then told his mother he was thinking about killing himself. Instead, he got help. He was going to be okay. He'd been accepted to a good college and was building a better life. A life. One he would not have had, she believed, had he not heard that story on that night.

As storytellers, we impact untold numbers of people every time we tell, listen and teach. As storytellers, we impact untold numbers every time we give less than all we have, every time we don't listen, every time we turn away from the teaching moment.

We never know how our actions will be reflected back to us, only that they will.

K

Kindness

Kindness is my abiding value and is part of my storytelling practice. I strive to be kind to my audience, to those who hire me, to the narrative and to myself. This leads to some best practices I find easier to enact when I remind myself that they come out of kindness.

Being kind to the audience.
I try to craft my shows so they take my audience into account. I work to tell stories appropriate to the people listening and to what I may know about outside events, so my stories fit into the context of the event, the geography, and the world. And I acknowledge that the people are people. Things happen. If a baby cries, if a cell phone goes off, if someone walks out, I don't take it personally. I have no idea what the extenuating circumstances are.

Being kind to those who hire me.
Whenever I am hired, I make sure we all have reasonable expectations. I listen to their concerns and do my best to answer them and make sure they feel heard.

When I am hired to perform, I make sure I meet expectations in material, timing (I don't run long or short if at all possible) and venue. To do otherwise is to be disrespectful to the event planner relying on me.

When I am hired to coach or teach, I use kindness as my first principle. I present new ideas in ways that are accessible. I listen and I support. The dissection and discussion can come after the value of the work is affirmed.

When I am hired to work with an organization I strive to discover as much as possible about the current state of morale, engagement and so on, so I can be kind to the people who take the workshop by understanding their situation and customizing my material for them. I want to meet their needs and the needs of those who hire me.

Being kind to the narrative.
I make sure I understand why I'm drawn to a particular story and then honor it. I try to make sure its roots are not forgotten, I get permission to tell a piece if it's crafted by another artist, I tell it to audiences who I think will appreciate it.

K

Being kind to myself.

I get listened to and try to minimize my own isolation. This helps keep my self-doubt at bay and allows me to be kinder to myself when I make mistakes. I hydrate. I try to take care of my body. I try to be gentle with myself if I am feeling stressed. I do something good for myself every day, even if it's as simple as having an extra cup of tea.

When I perform, I take a moment to feel centered on stage so I don't feel anxious. I ask for changes in the house lights so my eyes don't hurt. I do what I need to feel connected to the audience. I take my time.

K

Listening

There was a wonderful radio program on NPR called *This I Believe*, in which various people wrote and read essays on their core beliefs. These ranged from forgiveness to science to faith and more. I would listen to these essays, transfixed. I was moved to write my own *This I Believe* essay; I wrote more than one, as I found I have several core beliefs. But I kept coming back to the same things. Kindness. Compassion. Listening.

I believe in listening.

When asked to define myself, I often start with, "I am a listener."

This may seem like an odd thing for a storyteller to say. After all, my craft requires people to listen to me. Do I have to listen to them? Yes. When you think about it, storytelling starts with listening. Without a listener, the storyteller, no matter how superb, is talking to the wind. The wind may be an excellent listener, but because storytelling is an experience based on relationships, and most of us don't have two-way relationships with the wind, we need active and engaged listeners. Storytellers listen to their audiences while they tell their stories and shape the tale to meet the needs of the audience. It's a relationship, a dance, not just a rote performance.

Storytellers who listen to the world around them in their daily lives can craft stories that are more readily recognizable, where the audience can find themselves and their own story with more ease. These stories, where the audience doesn't have to work as hard, give the storyteller a way to reach their listeners and connect with them more deeply, thus creating a more satisfying experience to all. We're more likely to remember a story where we found ourselves, in some way, than a story we found completely alien. As it turns, out, we're all Luke Skywalker, Sleeping Beauty, and The Big Bad Wolf.

There's more to it than that. We all must be listeners to the world. When we listen intently to those around us, we have a much better chance of understanding them. We also model for them the way we want to be listened to. Have you ever had a conversation with someone where you were interrupted constantly, where that person kept diverting the conversation to themselves? Where your experiences were only launching pads to their own stories? We have a chronic listening deficit in the western world (maybe globally, I don't know). We are taught from a very young age that if we shut up and listen, we're passive, giving up the advantage, that we will gain nothing from the interaction. I disagree. By listening to those around me, by giving those with the greatest need to talk a chance to be heard, I have forged deep and meaningful relationships, helped people find their place in the world, and ultimately had opportunities to express my own ideas in a wider range of forums than I would have otherwise.

Listening is the base of every workshop I teach; it's inevitably the hardest part for participants. Being still and listening to others is harder than standing up and telling a story, harder than finding a new company vision, harder than working through your own life for your next story. Without listening, without being listened to and listening to others carefully, these tasks become much more challenging.

We can learn to be better listeners, it's a skill like any other.

Next time you're talking with someone you love, just listen to them. Don't interrupt with a question or your opinion, just pay attention and listen. Wait until they wind down before you praise, ask, or empathize. You may learn something you never knew.

Try just letting the interrupter talk. Listen to them. You may find they wind down after a while and become your ally because you are the person who took the time to hear them.

Listen to those whose views you oppose. You may find they have the same basic concerns that you do. They love their families, care about their communities and want to be happy just as much as you do. By listening to them you may teach them that the enemy isn't so frightening after all. If you can extend them that kindness maybe they can extend it back to you.

Leaders need to be great listeners. They must remember that everyone in their organization has their own measure of wisdom and opinion. By listening to them you may learn things you never knew about process, engagement, success or failure and potential improvement. But you must be willing to listen.

It's difficult. We want to share our own stories and have our own voice. You will have that chance, but if you can listen, you may learn more about the world and yourself than you ever expected.

Love

Some time ago my then-apprentice told to her largest audience yet. I was there to support her. She was nervous. Shortly before the performance, I asked her to look at the audience. "Really look," I said, "What do you see?"

"People staring at me."

"And?"

"Listeners?"

"And?"

"Just... people."

"People with the same hopes and fears you have. Love them and you won't have anything to be nervous about. Just love them."

Remember that our essential job as tellers is to leave the audience enthralled not only with us but with the story and its meaning in their lives. We must love them enough to be willing to let them immerse themselves in the storytelling experience and perhaps experience something different from what we intended. Our goal is to be so good at what we do that the audience can claim the story as relating to their own experience, regardless of whether it's a personal story, a traditional tale, fiction or another kind of narrative, and give it their own meaning. We are the messenger and the message. We must be willing to let the audience build their own world and that world may or may not have much to do with us. We must be able to let the audience develop their own relationship with the story.

I find it easier to give the audience space when I remind myself of several things.

◆ **We don't know what's going on inside the mind of a listener.** All we can do is offer them something that we know has meaning and trust them to take what they need,

◆ **This is easier to do when we approach our audience with love.** We don't punish babies for having needs, we recognize those needs and do our best to meet them. Likewise, with the audience. We may not know what those needs are, but we can admit they exist and leave room for them in our narrative by not demanding that the audience see every detail the way we do, instead constructing their own version in their own minds.

◆ **The act of storytelling becomes a gift** that can leave an audience transformed if there is room in the narrative for not only the teller and the tale but the listeners. In design, this is called white space. It is the space in which images, form and narrative structure exist, but with enough room that the audience isn't crowded out. It is the silence between notes in music. Without white space, meaning can be lost in the crowd. Don't worry, your audience will remember that you are the one who gave them space and permission to live in the moment of the story.

Storytelling is composed of relationships between the teller, the tale and the audience. When the teller loves the audience enough to let them form their own relationship with the tale, we can't help but transcend the moment. As listeners, we are moved beyond our everyday experiences into new worlds. As tellers, we become the sacred vessel that the best art is: a vehicle for transformation and connection between artist, art, audience and the world.

L

Love stories

Humans are fascinated with romantic love, commitment, and procreation. Mythology is full of love stories: Cupid and Psyche, Achilles and Patroclus, Rachel and Jacob, Krishna and Radha, Arthur and Guinevere and Lancelot. Our folktales are consumed with love and marriage. Our films, all musical genres, books, and popular media are obsessed with it. Who and how we love matters, we love talking about it, dreaming about it, telling stories about it.

There are some points to consider when telling love stories.

◆ **Personal, real-life love stories are very powerful for the audience to hear.** They may identify more easily with you, the teller, and the other characters if they believe this is a real-life (or close to real-life) experience.

  ❖ Has enough time passed since the incident that you can tell the story without the audience having to worry about you or you having to worry about the consequences? If you fall apart during your story about a breakup, then the audience is wrenched out of their own imaginations and into concern about you. Your job as a storyteller is to help them stay in that story-trance. If you can't yet tell that without sobbing, work on the story more or wait a bit longer.

  ❖ If you tell a real-life love story, decide how much information you should reveal or conceal. If the story is about real people, would they mind you talking about them? If your parents met in a strip club and this is a closely guarded family secret, shave off the serial numbers a little.

  ❖ Your passion becomes the audience's passion. There is a great deal of difference between, "We broke up," and "I loved them so much. It was so good for so long. And then something happened." Use your emotions to build the narrative.

◆ **If you're telling a myth or folktale, don't strip the passion out of it. Tell it like it's real.** These stories have stuck around for a long time because they talk about some of the basic parts of being human.

  Isis' quest to restore the body of her husband Osiris is full of love and sex, jealousy and triumph, pain and loneliness, feelings we may think of as very modern, yet the story is thousands of years old. When you tell these stories, they are your story. They speak of your own experiences in metaphoric language so you can infuse them with your own love, longing, pain, and jealousy.

◆ **Use sex appropriately.** Sex can be a part of love and so it may have a place in our love stories. If your story has sex scenes make sure you've practiced and are

L

comfortable telling them. Do your best to gauge your audience. For many audiences, an implied moment is far more meaningful and comfortable than a more thoroughly described one. Generally, with love stories, you don't want to knock your listeners out of their story trance by making them embarrassed.

◆ **Everyone has similar experiences.** The details of your love story will vary and will be utterly unique to you, but almost all of us have loved, longed and lost in our lives. By telling these stories we connect with one another, we comfort each other, we are permitted to feel just a little bit more than we might otherwise allow ourselves.

As storytellers, we are the ambassadors of human experience. Regardless of the kinds of stories we tell – but especially stories of basic experiences like love – we offer our listeners a chance to feel less alone, more connected and more alive. We heal ourselves and others by telling love stories and offering the hope that we, too, will be loved.

Marketing and branding

Marketing is the stuff you do to let others know about you and your work. This can include ads, articles, websites, business cards, etc. Anything you do to get word about you and your work into the world falls under marketing.

Marketing can be hard for storytellers to do effectively. It's easy to think that if you're a good storyteller people will naturally want to hear you but it doesn't work like that. People want to hear the storytellers they know about, and they don't know about you (let alone that you're good) if they don't know about you in the first place. Marketing is all the different ways you let people know you exist, such as a website, flyers, ads, etc.

Branding is a subset of marketing; it acts as a shorthand for potential customers to let them know that they are looking at *your* work and offerings, no one else's. Think about it. A pair of sneakers without a logo is just a pair of shoes. If it has the logo of A Big Name Show Company, then you are purchasing the company's promise these sneakers embody everything that Big Name Shoe Company stands for. It's the same with your branding. Branding is the promise to your customers (and that can be event organizers, audiences, etc.) that you will bring your own, special touch to the performance and that they are not getting anything less.

Branding is the thing that lets people know they are looking at *your* website, hearing *your* stories, etc.

Branding can include but is not limited to:

◆ How you dress when performing
◆ Catchphrases
◆ Logos
◆ Colors
◆ Fonts
◆ Any other way you establish your image in your customer's eyes.

Once you have a clear image of your brand, you can use it in all of your marketing. When you run an ad for your next performance, include your logo and catchphrase. If you develop a handout, use the colors and fonts you've selected. Your business cards should represent your brand.

Your work is good enough and you believe in it enough that it is a gift to the world to share it with others. Effective marketing and branding will make it easier to share and by doing so you will help build a better world.

Microphones, amplification, and stage lighting

It's nice to imagine every storytelling experience as being so intimate and connected that we need not use a microphone or be illuminated, but that's just not how it works. It's a good idea to familiarize yourself with how to use a microphone and take advantage of amplification and get used to stage lights.

◆ **Do a sound check whenever possible.** This means you have a chance to figure out if the settings are good for your voice, you can test the mic and speakers for the loud and soft ranges of your story, you can determine how close you should be to the mic itself.

◆ **Have an ally listen to your sound check.** You don't know what you'll sound like in the back of the hall. Test the quiet parts of the story and the loud. You may have to lower the volume on the louder parts when you are on a microphone. It always helps to have someone else there listening.

◆ **Most mics have a sweet spot.** If you're over six inches away, you may sound echoey or muted, if you're too close every sound in your mouth is amplified.

◆ **Know where the edges of your light are.** Do a lighting check so you know where you are illuminated. It may seem you are standing in the light, but stage lights can be deceiving, so ask someone to let you know what parts of the stage are brightest.

◆ **Stage lights can be blinding.** If you haven't worked with stage lighting before, be forewarned that it can be blinding. You may not be able to see the audience and you may not even know where the edges of the stage are.

◆ **Consider asking if the houselights can be raised just a little bit.** A small boost in the house lights makes it much easier for you to see some of your audience. You may not see them all clearly, but having at least outlines and silhouettes can make it easier to connect with them.

◆ **The audience will think you are looking at them even if you can't see them.** Once you're familiar with this, it makes using stage lights much easier. The audience will still feel connected to and seen by you, even if you can't see them clearly.

Monsters

Oh, but there are monsters in the world! Storytellers can talk about monsters, real and imagined, in safer ways, venturing to the edge of the world and back. We can conjure kraken and werewolves and vampires and ghosts just as easily as we talk about real-life monsters.

Whenever I tell a story with a monster in it, I ask myself:

◆ *Who really is the monster?* Imagine how that poor, hungry wolf felt, being denied a meal by those greedy pigs. Maybe Goldilocks is really a story about a home invasion. If my monster is the expected villain, I still try to understand them. Are they simply evil? Are they angry? What's going on?

◆ *What is the monster's point of view?* It can be very interesting, exploring the story from the other side. Telling the story from the monster's POV but letting it remain monstrous is an interesting challenge, one worth exploring if you have the time.

◆ *Where does the monster belong?* Maybe my listeners never need to see the monster, the threat might be enough.

◆ *When do I want to reveal the monster?* How terrifying is it once revealed?

◆ *Does the monster change as the story progresses?* Do I want to build sympathy for it or do I want it to remain terrible?

◆ *Ultimately, why is the monster there?* What would happen if I told the story without the monster in it? Would it still get my point across?

When I tell a story with a real-life monster, I may need to do some internal work to make sure I'm ready to tell it. It doesn't help if my fear of my third-grade bully is still making me shake. I need to make the bully terrifying, sure, but I also must make the bully as real for the audience as the fear is. If the monster is subtle – say a problem at work or an intractable situation – then I must make sure I set it carefully in its context.

There are standard monsters – ghosts, goblins, ghoulies, giants (and other things that don't start with g), etc., but I also sometimes consider if there might be a hidden monster in a story. If I'm telling Demeter's story, is her grief monstrous? Does it drive her to do terrible things? If I think of the grief as its own monstrous character, how does the story change? What if I'm the monster?

We are surrounded by monsters. We often are monsters. As storytellers, we explore the darkness with narrative as our torch. If you know your monsters inside and out, your telling will be richer, more believable and your audience will more willingly venture into the unknown, here-there-be-monsters places with you.

Movement and gesture

There is no one right way to move when you tell stories. What matters is that you are aware of your movements and gestures and that they are deliberate so they won't distract the audience.

It's a good idea to put some thought into the space around you and how you move through it. You can, for instance, plot out different parts of the stage as representing different parts of the story. This is especially useful if you are telling a story from multiple points of view. You may not have that flexibility if you're using a stand mic, but you must still think about what you do with your hands. I have seen good stories diminished because the storyteller didn't know what to do with their hands while they were telling, so they held them as if they were holding a melon in front of them throughout the telling. It was distracting. Think about using your pockets, letting your hands rest at your sides, or even hold onto the mic.

M

A good way to check your movements and gestures is to watch a video of yourself telling. It might be difficult, but it's worth noticing distracting motions and effective ones.

Movement and gesture can add immensely to the story if they are considered. They can distract terribly if they are not. Take some time to see how other tellers move, watch your own videos, and remember that your whole body tells the tale. Let it speak eloquently.

Narrator's voice and point of view

We assume all different kinds of roles when we tell our stories. As the performer, we are also the narrator of the tale, whether we are telling a true story in the first person, or a traditional piece in third. There are many different kinds of narrators and points of view, each has their own strengths and concerns. When you understand who your narrator is and how to use their voice, you can tell your story more effectively and consistently.

The narrator's voice differs from the viewpoint. It's more about the performance choices a storyteller makes than plot and structure. It's *how* you tell the story. For instance, you could tell The Three Little Pigs as a secondary character, the first person from a variety of points of view, including the mother, the wolf, or another character you create, but you would still use the same narrator's voice – secondary character, first person. Viewpoint defines the narrating character, it's *who* tells the story. The viewpoint can be expressed through the narrator voice but it may not define it.

- **Protagonist, first person**
  We use this voice whenever we tell a story from the protagonist's viewpoint using first person (I, me). Common examples include many story slam stories or fractured fairy tales told from the main character's viewpoint. The protagonist is the focus of the story.

- **Protagonist, third person**
  Narration in she/he voice but restricted to the main character's understanding of the story. For example, a third person telling of Cinderella in which all the action is within her understanding of the world.

- **Secondary character, first person, lead POV**
  A secondary character (the wolf for example) tells the story in the first person from their viewpoint

- **Secondary character, first person, observer POV**
  A secondary character (the wolf for example) tells the story of the protagonist in the first person from their outside viewpoint. For example, the fairy godmother tells Cinderella's story, with Cinderella being the focus.

- **Secondary character, third person**
  Narration in s/he voice but restricted to a secondary character's viewpoint. For instance, the story of Snow White is typically told in protagonist, third person. It could be told in secondary character, third person, if you related the woodsman's story.

- **Omniscient narrator, largely third person**
  Differs from Protagonist, third person, because the narrator can relate things the protagonist may not know.

- **Commentator narrator, largely third person with first person asides**

  Third person narration (s/he) but the teller occasionally will insert first person, personal commentary. Many Russian fairy tales are told in the third person with commentary at the end such as, "And I know this story is true because the wine stained my beard red!" *A Christmas Carol* is a literary example.

- **Secret narrator, third person until the end**

  Appears to be a third person narration until the end, when character voice switches into first. This is an effective technique to drive a point home, to reveal something about the narrator more powerful in the first person, and so on.

- **Unreliable narrator, usually though not always first person**

  A narrator who cannot be trusted. Often the unreliable narrator lets the audience know they are unsure of events or flat out lying, though it could be revealed at the end that the narrator was untruthful or was themselves deceived and what they thought happened, didn't. Often used in suspenseful or scary stories to heighten uncertainty.

- **Second person**

  Narration using "you" as the pronoun of choice. This isn't a common occurrence in performance storytelling but can be done. It places the audience in the role of the protagonist. It can quickly become difficult to follow plot if the story isn't carefully crafted.

N

Neurology of storytelling: Why it works

Humans evolved to understand the world through shared, oral stories. It makes sense when you think about it. We've been telling stories for millennia while we've been reading on a large scale for, maybe, a thousand years and video is only a hundred years old. Our brains are wired for story.

I could spend the rest of this book waxing poetic about the neurology of storytelling, but instead, let me share with you the five most powerful research-based aspects of the brain on story.

◆ Oral storytelling makes the brain engage in **neural coupling**, which means that if you hear a story about a particular activity, say running or having a particular emotion, the brain behaves as if it is experiencing that activity. This allows the listener to turn the story into their own ideas and experience, so they will care more about it and are more invested in acting upon the information the story provides.

◆ When processing facts alone, two areas of the brain are most active: Broca's and Wernicke's areas. These parts of the brain are associated with processing language. When we hear a story with a narrative and emotional rise and fall, the **whole brain is engaged** including the motor cortex, sensory areas (vision, hearing, smell, touch, etc.) and the frontal cortex.

◆ People who hear a story experience **brain mirroring** which means they will experience similar brain activity to the speaker and to other listeners. You will feel and react in similar ways to those around you. This is part of what makes motivational speaking and political speeches so effective.

◆ Recent research suggests that stories are stored in the brain as if they are **memories**. That means that a well-told story will be remembered as if it happened to the listener (even if they know it didn't) in emotional power and persuasiveness.

◆ When someone hears a story with emotional content, blood levels of the **hormones** dopamine (associated with memory) and oxytocin (associated with empathy and emotional connection) radically increased. Our brains want to remember and build relationships based on the story.

All of this together means that storytelling is as close to telepathy and mind-melding as we have. It is a powerful, persuasive tool that builds empathy and relationships between listeners and tellers at the speed of thought.

No

I love performing. I love the connection with the audience, the rush as I see them lean into the story, the chatter afterward. It's exhilarating and addictive. I must be careful though; like any addiction, my desire for performance can lead to bad choices. I remind myself there are times when I should say *no* to a gig.

I have made the mistake of taking gigs I wasn't the best teller for. I have found myself in front of wiggling 2-year-olds and thought *I don't know what to do here*. I've taken gigs I knew would be emotionally difficult. I'd like to think I have learned something from these experiences, because now I am much more willing to say, "No, thank you, I'm not the right teller for you but so-and-so is." It's hard to do. Every single time a part of me cringes and fears I will never get more work, but when I say no to a gig I am not suited for, I am creating space for those that suit me best and behaving with an attitude of abundance.

Think of it this way, no one can be everything to everyone. Chefs specialize. Firemen specialize. Dancers and writers specialize. Professors, garbage men, politicians, librarians, construction workers, teachers, painters... I cannot name a field where there is not some specialization. I think it's hard for storytellers to do this because storytelling is such a basic part of what it is to be human: We all tell stories. So those of us who do it professionally should be able to do it all, right? Wrong. None of us are superb in every aspect of this art.

When we take that bold path of recognizing that we are not suited for a particular gig (whether it's personal circumstances, training, natural inclination, or for other reasons) we create several positive effects.

- We **raise the standards of our art** by making sure our audiences hear great stories suited for them so those who hire us have a deeper appreciation for the art.
- We **build deeper relationships** with our fellow tellers by being generous and giving them the chance to be generous in the future.
- We have an opportunity to **increase our skill set**. If we know we're not ready now we can learn more and be ready in the future. If you're not comfortable telling to preschoolers, take a class and volunteer at the local homeless shelter. They need the stories and you need the practice.
- Sometimes we just need to admit we aren't prepared to **devote ourselves fully** to what is a very demanding art form. Would you run a marathon without training?

I know this may be hard to imagine, but I have found that by turning down gigs for which I am not suited, I get more gigs for which I am the best suited. It sounds a little mystical maybe, but there it is.

Storytelling requires us to be mindful and honest with ourselves and our audiences. Isn't that a basic part of what storytelling is about anyway, authentic joy in the art and connection with the audience? No one would choose this path if they weren't passionate about it, it's too much work, so do the work you are passionate about and help others do it too by giving them the chances you don't need.

A place for your thoughts.

Optimism and opportunity

We never know when a chance to tell stories will come upon us. I have found myself unexpectedly telling stories on public transit, in business meetings, in hospital, on airplanes, and to random strangers on the street. We never know when the universe will say *Here. Now. Tell a story. Here is an opportunity to share.* We must pay attention to these opportunities and be ready when they arise. Don't be afraid.

What's more, we never know when we will be given the gift of story fodder, the opportunity to craft a story out of the world around us. It might be in the overheard conversation, in a moment inspired by a book or movie, in the time spent with strangers or loved ones. We never know when the universe will say *Shut up. Listen. Here is an opportunity to hear something magnificent.* We must pay attention to these opportunities and remember that storytelling starts with listening.

Beyond opportunities to remember we live in a world rich with story that needs ours as much as anyone else's, we also never know when we will have an opportunity for work. It could arise out of a casual conversation, a referral, almost anything. We just must remember to be grateful and to be ethical in the work we do because we never know when the universe will say *Try this. You'll be great.* We must pay attention to these opportunities, strive to make them and accept them when they arise. And, because the universe sometimes needs a bit of help, carry business cards.

This reminds me of a joke.

There was a great flood and a man found himself stranded on the roof of his home. He prayed, asking God to rescue him. After a few minutes, some people in a canoe came along and invited him in. "No," he replied, "I'm fine. God will take care of me."

He kept praying. The water kept rising. It lapped at the edges of the roof.

Soon some people in a rowboat drifted by and asked if he needed help. "No," he replied, "I'm fine. God will take care of me."

He kept praying. The water kept rising. Now the water was as high as his toes.

Soon a helicopter hovered over him. They threw down a ladder and called out, "Climb on!" "No," he replied, "I'm fine. God will take care of me."

The helicopter roared away. He kept praying. The water kept rising. The house shuddered and then it collapsed underneath him. Try as he might, he soon drowned.

The man found himself in Heaven. He asked God, "Why didn't you help? I prayed!"
And God replied, "Hey, I sent two boats and a helicopter, what more did you want?"

The storyteller's work fits in just about anywhere. We just need to pay attention and the opportunities are there.

Organizational storytelling

Why do organizations need storytelling? At its most basic, organizations need stories because people need them. Human beings have been understanding the world through story for as long as we have been people. Since organizations are comprised of, managed and invented by, work for and serve people, organizations need stories.

What can an effective storytelling practice do for your organization? Lots. To start with:

Internally, storytelling can:

◆ Build a better culture
◆ Identify issues before they become big problems
◆ Help solve those problems in new and creative ways
◆ Talk about the tough stuff safely
◆ Ensure all stakeholders are heard
◆ Preserve organizational history
◆ Act as a change agent
◆ Help you plan and set goals creatively
◆ Perpetuate your brand
◆ Clarify your vision, mission, and values

Externally, storytelling can:

◆ Convey your brand and message more effectively than traditional methods
◆ Engage your customers, clients and fans in a dialogue that gets them more invested
◆ Set your organization's goals into a real-world context, beyond facts and figures
◆ Offer far more compelling presentations, campaigns, and fund-raising pitches
◆ Talk about the tough stuff in realistic, humane and well-crafted ways
◆ Share your culture, history, mission, and values
◆ Explore your role in the word by listening to the stories told about your organization
◆ Position your organizations as one that understands and values your impact on people
◆ Guide through hard times by drawing on the past to build the future
◆ Create change by changing the story

This is just a start. Because humans have always told stories – we are, in fact, wired for a story – it is a versatile and important tool. Organizations that value narrative and storytelling are capitalizing on one of the basic things that make us human. We all tell stories. Together we can figure out how to tell better stories that have a greater impact and make the world a better place.

A place for your thoughts.

Personal storytelling and what to reveal

My late husband and storytelling partner-in-crime Kevin Brooks told personal stories long before it was fashionable. Decades ago he was mining his own life for material and crafting stories that were funny, poignant and meaningful. He often said that God had given him a crazy family as material for storytelling. He didn't hesitate.

I was amazed. At the time I couldn't imagine telling stories about my own life, let alone the lives of my friends and family. It seemed too revealing, too personal. I preferred to tell truths masked in metaphor. We had many long conversations about the ethics of telling stories in which other people's truth are revealed. He was adamant that 1) these stories were important, that people needed to hear them; 2) that no one was harmed even if he told something embarrassing; and 3) that I should tell personal stories, too. Kevin insisted this was one of the risks of having a storyteller in the family; nothing was sacred and everything could be revealed.

It took a while, but eventually, I began to tell personal stories, tales that involve my friends and family. I struggled with what to reveal and what to conceal. I still do.

The joy of telling personal stories is that your life is constantly generating material to share. Audiences love hearing true stories (or at least stories that are mostly true) because it gives them something to identify with. It helps build bridges and connect us.

P

Personal storytelling is everywhere. It's the dominant form of performance storytelling. The telling of personal stories is so powerful (at least in part) because it reminds us we are not alone. None of us is entirely unique in the universe and when we hear someone tell a story about an experience that echoes our own, no matter how strange or traumatic, we connect.

As a performing storyteller, I must have at least a few personal stories in my repertoire, but it's important that I respect the people who appear in them. I don't want to insult or betray my friends and family if I tell stories about them that are less than complimentary, yet those are the stories I sometimes need to tell.

I manage this by asking them when I can, by changing names and other identifying details or, in the rare occasion when the story cannot be changed yet is important enough to still tell, forging ahead with it but being careful about where I tell it. I know I am more sensitive to this than many. In general, I have found people are delighted when I tell stories about them.

Kevin once gave his mother a stack of stories he'd written about her. She read them for a long time, staying in one place, each page slowly moving from the unread stack to the read. He was nervous; buried in there was a story about an old family secret in which she took revenge on an unfaithful suitor. He waited. And waited. After a while, it was clear she had passed that story. He was about to ask her what she thought when he noticed her shoulders were shaking. She looked up and tears were streaming down her face. She was laughing so hard she could make no noise and her eyes were watering.

When she finally caught her breath, she reached toward him and choked out, "It's all true! It's all true!"

I think this may be the secret to telling stories about our friends and family.
Tell the truth.
Maybe wait a little while until the rawness has healed.
Remember that we storytellers are speakers of the truth.
We build a connection.
We drive away shadows.
One story at a time, we heal the world.

P

Personal vs. traditional stories

The popularity of personal storytelling is soaring. Venues like The Moth have brought thousands upon thousands of new listeners to one of the oldest art forms. It's thrilling, yet it can be frustrating for those who tell traditional stories and aren't interested in telling the personal. Let's look at the pros and cons of personal and traditional telling and see what common ground we can find.

Let's start with a tiny bit of history.

◆ People have been telling stories for as long as we have been people. I expect this includes both "personal" (real, first person) stories and "traditional" (metaphoric or fictional) stories.

◆ About 40 years ago storytelling festivals began to appear in the United States. They may well have existed for longer in the U.S. and longer in other countries, but I'm recounting the history as I know it.

◆ In the late 1990s, the Moth launched in New York City, which focuses on personal narrative.

◆ By the mid-2000s, story slams were proliferating and festivals were experiencing declines in attendance.

This set up some apparent conflict between storytellers who leaned towards traditional stories and those who came up through the slam scene or otherwise leaned towards personal stories. There is a lot of grumbling on both sides about relative value.

I find this grumbling to be unfortunate and divisive. There is power and value to both forms of narrative and each can learn from the other. I also suspect some of it is generational. I know I sometimes feel like an old geezer, frustrated that everyone thinks this stuff is new and has no interest in the fact that I've been doing it for decades, but those are just feelings. When I step out of my discontent, I'm sure there is room and need for both.

Definitions

It might be useful to have clear working definitions of "personal" and "traditional" story-telling. These definitions are for this book and so start with the assumption that we're talking about live performance without a script-in-hand, operating on the principles of the story triangle. With that in mind, I define "personal storytelling" as first-person narra-tive that the audience believes recounts something that happened to the individual tell-ing it or someone they know, something that's more-or-less true; first person, nonfiction, personally experienced. I define "traditional storytelling" as first or third person narrative, recounting a story with roots in the oral tradition that the audience believes is fictional and metaphorical; first or third person, fiction, not personally experienced.

I'm setting up these parameters because there are worlds of story that don't fall into either category (fiction, literary, historical, etc.). These other categories are wonderful and important, but I'll set them aside for now. I want to work with the clearer forms I just described.

Cultural role and meaning
Both traditional and personal narratives have important cultural roles. Like all stories, they give us a chance to look at our own lives and actions through a narrative lens. We hear or tell a story and relate our own experience to it.

Traditional stories use metaphors. These stories give us a chance to interpret signs and symbols for deeper meaning. They often carry cultural knowledge about morals, danger, ethics and so on. When we tell or hear a traditional narrative, we can scratch under the surface, find the author's intended meaning and decide how we wish to interpret the same material. Is Red Riding Hood about ignoring your mother? Talking to strangers? Puberty? Delivering goodies to the infirm? There is a potential openness to the narrative that is both empowering and isolating. We are given the tools to make our own meaning but often must make meaning for the story to make sense. We need to stretch further sometimes, to accept a world with talking animals and clearly defined morals. We need to accept that the symbols have meaning and that the teller makes it worth it for us to suspend our disbelief. If we don't, then the story may not be engaging.

Personal narrative (as defined above) doesn't need a metaphor. These stories are recounting true events with the meaning sometimes explicitly described in the narrative (I learned that the woods are dangerous) and other times left open for the listeners to entirely fabricate (I never went to my grandmother's house again). Because the narrative is assumed to be factual the cultural meaning exists in the actions and words of the story, not in the hidden meaning behind them. The hidden meaning may be there if the author crafts it in, but it isn't required. We may find it easier to empathize with these stories because they don't require the stretch of metaphor; the meaning may be easier to find. We must be willing to believe the teller and let whatever they say relate to our own lives simply, without symbolic trappings. If we are not inclined to find ourselves in others' lives, these stories will be less engaging.

Historically, traditional stories were (among other things) teaching tools. We told and heard these tales to understand our world without having to put ourselves directly into risky situations, they helped us through different stages of our lives. Personal narrative can do the same thing, although much of the prevalent form of personal storytelling seems built more on the extraordinary, so these stories don't require interpretation or offer as much as teaching tools but provoke empathy and may help build a connection. Maybe traditional stories are more about the communal learning/hearing experience, while personal tales are more about the sense of not being alone because of the empathy provoked by the story itself.

The story triangle
Both forms of narrative rely on the story triangle for their power. The interaction between teller, tale, and audience is very much at play as these stories are performed.

Personal stories well-told allow us to gasp in awe at the lives of others. Depending on the tale and teller, there may not be as much room for the listener's interpretation, but these stories help us build bridges across culture, class and ethnic boundaries. We all have had crummy times, adventures, loss and triumph. Hearing another's story at the least reminds us we are not alone.

Traditional stories require more meaning-making, something that I think is not in great vogue these days. Nonetheless, when hearing a well-told traditional tale, we can marvel at the power of our own imaginations, touch other cultures and maybe learn a little about how to move through the world. Some of the oldest stories remind us that we all have a commonality of experience and, at the least, reminds us that we are not alone. Fictional stories, like a traditional narrative, can also give the listener and teller a psychological distance that may make it easier to observe, analyze, reveal, and critique.

It may be that traditional stories are more about the communal learning/hearing experience, while personal tales are more about the sense of not being alone because of the empathy provoked by the story itself.

So what do I think?
If you've gotten this far then you know that I think both forms of story have value. The current cultural love for personal narrative isn't surprising; we live in a voyeuristic society where the selfie matters and gossip-based websites add to our hunger for personal anecdotes. I think it's misleading to say that traditional stories have lost value, we need only look at other forms of storytelling to remember that traditional material still resonates (films, tv shows, etc.).

The problem may come down to segregation. Personal story events draw listeners because they know what to expect; true(ish) stories that show their peers as fallible, heroic, tragic. These are the same qualities they find in themselves, only exposed and well-articulated. If these audiences are never exposed to well-chosen traditional material that includes the fallible, heroic and tragic, why should they ever come to a traditional event? If someone loves fairy tales why would they think they might find meaning in a coming-of-age tale? We, as storytellers and organizers, need to market our material wisely. What if a story slam included a special teller who told a short, funny, ribald traditional story? What if someone known for traditional material included a story about their personal life? Both stories could echo the theme of the event.

There was a time that I refused to tell personal stories; it felt like an invasion of my privacy. Then I remembered a quote from the filmmaker Frederico Fellini, "All art is autobiographical." With that, I realized that the traditional stories I told were meaningful because I gave them meaning. It no longer was frightening to tell personal tales or make a fairy tale personal. Now I tell more stories, connect with more audiences and learn more about the craft every day.

One other thought is about merging genres. Since I began telling professionally, I have told fairy tales as if they were personal stories and woven magic into my personal stories. Both traditional and personal stories offer the teller the chance to examine their own lives; both tools have value; exploring the ground in between may yield marvelous new art that is accessible, meaningful, and imaginative.

Let's end with a story.
Once upon a time, there were two siblings living on an island. This island had two tall peaks and a flat valley. One day they stood in the valley and looked to the ocean where they saw the dark line of an incoming tsunami.
"Quick! Climb my mountain!" said one sibling.
"Mine is taller, climb this one!"
The siblings stood in the valley, shouting at one another. The roar of the tsunami grew.

What if we recognized that all stories, regardless of traditional, personal, or other, have value when they are well told, when there is room for the audience and when we remember that stories are about human experience, whether true or metaphorical? What if festivals opened themselves more to slams, personal narrative along with traditional material? What if slams opened the door for less-than-true tales? What if we opened that door for all listeners and gave them a chance to experience a broader world of story? What if we decided that both mountains are tall enough?

Practice

You know how to get to Carnegie Hall, right? Practice.

It's easy, in the first flush of falling in love with storytelling and the audience, to forget that we need to apply as much time and practice to our art as any other artist does. Because so much of we do is about connecting with the audience, many novice tellers hope we don't need to work, craft, and practice before we get up on stage, that talent and charisma will carry the day. This isn't true. Like all other artists, storytellers must craft, hone, and practice.

The best storytellers I know are diligent about practice. They work on their craft like they're building houses, starting from the foundation up, paying attention to every corner and window. It's work. It takes practice.

There are many ways you can practice your craft. I do these and I'm sure many other methods will work for you.

- **Write an outline.** Remove all the excess and tell only from the sparse notes.
- **Find a trusted friend and tell your story to them.** Ask them to tell you the things they love the most about the story.
- **Tell your story to a tree or the ocean, something that helps you listen more deeply to yourself.** You might hear things you didn't notice before.
- **Hold a small house concert.** Invite people who will be happy to hear a practice run. Wine might help.
- **Video yourself telling.** Then watch, so you can see what body language worked and what didn't. It might be difficult but it will help you become better at your art.
- **Hire a story coach or director.** They have experience and an eye that might be useful.
- **Go to an open mic and tell part of the piece there.** Nothing like having a live audience to help you along.

Your story may change as you practice. Let it. These changes might be great new facets you never explored. Don't be afraid to let parts fall by the wayside. It doesn't mean they're bad, just that they might belong somewhere else.

P

Remember that each telling experience is a chance to practice. Because storytelling is such a flexible art, your story will change with each telling, but practice means you know the rhythms of the story. You know the hard places. You know how audiences tend to react and you're prepared when they react in new ways or you are interrupted.

Practice is just a chance to tell your story again. Enjoy yourself. Enjoy your storytelling practice. And isn't it grand we can always learn more about our art and craft!

P

Professionalism

Strictly speaking, professionalism is defined as the competence or skill expected of a professional. It also includes how we behave how we present ourselves, and how we talk about our peers, whether or not we make our living from the doing.

Storytellers, whether passionate amateur or working artist, should have standards of professionalism. This is part of having good working ethics. You don't have to be deeply experienced or a top-tier teller to present yourself professionally.

Know your material and prepare for your audience. Dress appropriately, whatever that means to you (though I wouldn't advocate wearing a swimsuit to a business presentation unless you checked first). Behave in a way that makes you and other storytellers look good. Arrive at your gig on time. Don't badmouth other tellers. These are all hallmarks of a professional, beyond your ability on the stage.

When you behave professionally (whether you are a working artist or not) you elevate the art for all of us. Organizers will hire you again because you're easy to work with, your colleagues will speak well of you, and your audiences will love your work.

P

Props, puppets, and other story aids

It can be fun to use a prop or a puppet when performing. It sometimes adds a whole new depth to the piece and may delight your audience. Some storytellers use origami or balloon animals to enhance their work. As with any part of being a performing artist, make sure you can use it well before taking it in front of the audience. The prop should enhance and support you and the story, not become the main attraction because it isn't used well.

I have seen too many performers become more concerned about the state and use of their prop than the story. Suddenly our attention is on the thing, not the performer or the narrative. Likewise, I have seen puppets used badly. The performer doesn't know how to make the puppet look lively or they even move the puppet's mouth when the puppet character isn't speaking. It is distracting and can be confusing.

Please practice. Maybe even take a class or two so you have some training. Watch videos of other storytellers who use props well and ask your allies to help you become better at it by letting you know what works and what doesn't.

As with all aspects of the storyteller's craft, please know why you are using the prop and make sure you can use it well. You want it to enhance the performance, not distract from it.

P

Questions to ask yourself

I find it very helpful to ask myself all kinds of questions when I'm developing a story, workshop or class. After performing, consulting, teaching or coaching I ask myself questions to help me assess how it went. I ask my coaching clients questions to help them explore new avenues. Here are a just few examples of each.

Story development questions:

◆ Why does this story matter to me? What is, to borrow from storyteller and coach Doug Lipman, the most important thing?
◆ What do I want the audience to take away from it?
◆ Is it appropriate for me to tell this story?
◆ I might ask a friend to interview me as one of the characters, asking me questions that help me deepen the telling.
◆ Questions for coaching clients are similar.

Class, workshop or consulting questions:

◆ What have I been hired to do? What are the expectations I must meet?
◆ With whom will I be working? What level of expertise might they already have?
◆ Will I need to convince them this is worthwhile and, if so, what do I know about them already that could help?

Post-performance/event questions:

◆ Did the audience/students seem to get something out of it?
◆ Did I meet the set expectations? Did I exceed them?
◆ If something went awry, what can I learn from it?

A place for your thoughts.

Reconnecting

Sometimes I get grumpy and feel disconnected from my work. Does this ever happen to you? Do you ever just feel out of sorts because you have wandered away from the sources of your art? It happens more often than I care to admit because being a working artist is as much about marketing and administration as it is about creating. I understand that and I welcome the entire package. I wouldn't choose to live another life, but... sometimes it makes me really crabby.

When this happens, my first reaction is usually to run as hard and as fast as I can away from the things that will help. I want to watch mindless television, buy something, go to sleep. I want to feel numb rather than doing the things I need most because doing them will often make me feel more. When I finally stop running long enough to notice what I'm doing (and I run just about every time, it's amazing I create anything) I feel sheepish; kind of ashamed and relieved that probably no one noticed me running. Everyone else is too busy with their own avoidance runs to see mine most of the time.

Once I've caught my breath, I make a cup of tea and try to reconnect with myself enough to know what will help me through *this* moment of grumpiness, what will help me reconnect with my artistic source for just this moment. Once I manage one moment, I can often manage another and feel much better until the next time I disconnect. And I will disconnect again.

Here are a few things that help me reconnect to myself and my artistic passion. I'm sure you have your points of reconnection, too.

R

- ◆ Really, **I make myself a cup of tea**. But this time, I try to pay attention. I try to notice the water steeping, the color changing. I watch the swirls of milk. I let the flavor unfold on my tongue. I use this as a meditative moment and to be present. Sometimes I'll do something physical so I can feel the push and pull of my muscles, reminding me of my own strength.
- ◆ **I go back to the old stories.** I pull a real book off my shelf and read about Baba Yaga or Nasrudin or Jack. I remind myself of some of the universal truths about being human and connect with the stories I love.
- ◆ **I get listened to.** I find someone who cares about me and I tell them a story so I can remember that I am good at this. Sometimes I might invite several people over and put on a mini-concert. I remind myself of how whole I feel when I create and when I perform.

◆ **I write a love letter.** It might be to a person. It might be to a story. It might be to a tree. I sit down and remind myself specifically of why I love something or someone and detail it. This helps me connect with sensory imagery and emotional truth. I usually burn the letter afterward, though sometimes I will share it. And sometimes I try to write one to myself. This is much harder.

◆ **I take in art I love.** I go to a museum and look at a specific piece of art, one I've looked at before. I listen to Brahms or Chopin or Miles Davis. I read aloud a poem by someone whose words I love. I feel it in my mouth and bones.

◆ **I get away from the screen.** I try to write something by hand or hold a real book. I turn off my cell phone.

◆ **I spend time around others.** I might go to a cafe or someplace where other people are working so I feel more push to work on something, too. Peer pressure helps.

◆ **I spend time in nature.** I walk with trees or by the river. I remind myself that I am very small but as essential as *that* blade of grass or *this* ant. I am part of a whole.

All of this helps. It helps me to remind myself that everything I do has an impact. When I run, I have an impact on the world; I decrease myself and my place in it. When I create, when I listen, when I am present, my ripples are likely to be less violent and more connective. I'd rather connect. Most of the time, anyway.

R

Recording

Many performing storytellers offer recordings of their work for sale. Making a recording is a significant undertaking but need not be a difficult one. There are some questions to consider as you begin this process that will make it much easier.

◆ **Why do you want to make a recording?** Understand your reasons for wanting to make a recording. If it's mostly for marketing purposes, then you might pick different stories than you would if it were for posterity only.

◆ **Who is your audience?** Know who you want to listen to the recording. That will influence what stories you include and the packaging.

◆ **Who will record it for you?** It's important that your recording sound good. You want it to be professional so the people who listen to it don't have to strain to hear you and they know you cared enough to make sure it sounds good. Ask other storytellers who they used as their sound engineer.

◆ **What format will you use?** Many storytellers use CDs, some use USB drives or downloads. Ask around and see who sells what.

◆ **What is your budget?** Cost is always a factor. Each component has a cost, from recording to artwork to reproduction. Shop around to make sure you know what you can afford.

◆ **Live or in the studio?** Live recordings have a vitality that can be very engaging, but there isn't much room for error. A good studio recording can sound great and gives you more editing options. Think about which you prefer listening to and how much editing you think will be required.

◆ **Do you want sound effects?** Some storytellers use sound effects to enhance their stories. If you want to use them, talk with your sound engineer about how much emphasis you want to put on sound effects and which ones to use. They will have good advice.

R

Remembering the story

Some storytellers are advocates of memorizing your stories as if you were in a play. Generally speaking, I am not. I find if I know the structure of the story, key phrases, and important images, I can tell the story with more fluidity and more easily meet the needs of my audience.

First, I break the story into a fairly sparse outline. It contains the main plot points and structure of the story and little else. Then I add in key images I want to be consistent in each telling and add in key phrases. I practice telling the story from these bones.

For example, story bones of Little Red Riding Hood might look something like this:

- Little house in woods
- Girl, red hood
- Mom, a basket of goodies
- "Don't stray off the path"
- Big woods – light streaming through leaves
- Flowers
- Wolf
- Where? Grandma's
- Eats her, wears g-ma's clothing
- "What big eyes" – "All the better to see you with"
- Big ears – better to hear you with
- Big nose – better to smell you with
- Big teeth – better to eat you with!
- Warning re: wolves in the forest (always bring your cell phone)

Why do I prefer learning a story from an outline rather than memorizing? There are a few reasons. Honestly, I don't like memorizing things. I never have. More importantly, by remaining flexible with the language I use, I can customize each telling for each audience. Practically, the story is the same when I tell it to similar audiences because I've told it so often. A word or two may change, but it's almost identical to last time. Yet because it's not memorized, I can remain limber and responsive to each audience and set of circumstances. I am less likely to be thrown off by interruptions because it doesn't matter if I don't use the same words. I can be more responsive to the audience's needs. Should I make a mistake, because the story doesn't have to be identical each time I tell it, I can more easily weave my way back to the complete work.

Memorization may work for you. If that's the case, then go for it! Just remember, there are other ways of learning stories that might be useful, too.

Repertoire

While a storyteller shouldn't be judged solely by the size of their repertoire, it helps if you know enough stories that you can appeal to different audiences and ensure you have more than one set for repeat audiences. You may specialize in one kind of story but you want to know enough different stories that your repeat audience will hear more than one tale and more than one kind of story. You don't have to be a generalist with a repertoire of hundreds of stories, but you want to be able to accept confidently the gigs you are offered.

I recommend most storytellers know a handful of scary stories, personal stories, folktales, a myth or two, and a few participatory stories. You may be the master of epic narrative, but if you have a few extra minutes in a set, or if you're invited to be part of the ghost story concert at a festival, you want a trick or two up your sleeve.

Look for public domain material you enjoy. Tell the stories occasionally to keep them fresh and they will help you out in a pinch.

Equally, you must have stories in your repertoire that mean something to you, stories you know will move an audience, and (if you've been at it any length of time) stories you no longer tell.

Last, I hope you like the stories you tell. I hope you understand why they are in your repertoire beyond satisfying the requirements of a gig. I hope you keep learning new tales and enjoy them all.

R

Research

When I research a story, be it a myth, a folktale, a legend, a historical piece, the fact-based parts of original fiction or the details of a personal story, I give it greater depth. While my research might never make it into the final piece, it informs how I tell the story. If I know, for example, that my great-grandmother never got over the boyfriend she left behind in Russia, then that might color the way she talks to my grandmother about boys.

Good research shapes each character, setting, and event in your story. While it isn't a prerequisite to being a storyteller, when you love a piece you want to know more about it, so research is a natural side-effect.

It may feel like you don't know where to start with your research, but a simple online search or chat with the local librarian will get you started. You won't be graded, there is nothing to lose by digging in a little deeper.

R

Resilience

I'm sorry to tell you this, but you will have bad days as a storyteller. The audience won't show or they won't get your stories. You get a terrible review. You forget a gig and get the "where are you" call. You screw up a tale. Whatever it may be, sometimes you will think about throwing in the towel.

Don't do it. At least, don't do it right then, until you've had time to recover and assess what happened.

Storytellers (and all humans) need to be resilient. We must be able to take the bad stuff, then dust ourselves off and keep going. Sometimes we take a break before continuing the journey, but we keep going.

Resilient people are more able to manage the crap that life can throw at us and storytellers know resilience. We know the stories of worlds turned upside down and then gradually rebuilt. We know folktales of those who held on and solved problems, like Janet who held onto Tam Lin until he found his way home again. We know about the people who find a way to thrive despite adversity. Hope and life are possible, even when we go down to the underworld. We know resilience.

Learn what helps you be resilient and practice it, so when the time comes that you need it most, it is there. If you can practice not seeing every failure as catastrophic, every setback as the end, when you need to be able to take a breath and keep going, you can. You will.

R

Respect

Storytelling is about a lot of things. It's about being on stage. It's about being heard. It's about entertainment, about craft, about provoking a reaction. It's about developing a relationship with the audience and to do that, you must respect them.

It's easy to become jaded when you perform frequently and forget that each audience is unique with its own needs. It's easy to forget that your job is to meet those needs the best you can, each and every time you perform.

Every audience has similarities. Ideally, they are coming to your performance with an idea of what you are like and what they can expect. You can make some general assumptions that an audience of four-year-olds will have different needs from a festival crowd, which will have different needs from elders in an assisted living facility. It's our job as performing storytellers to pay attention to each audience, to respect them enough to do our best for them, each and every time.

Our best may vary, but if we remember that they are as hungry for recognition as we are, if we respect them enough, then we won't lose sight of their taking time out of their lives to pay attention to us. Admittedly, a given audience might do things that limit your ability to respect them but remember that the next audience is a new audience and just as deserving of respect at the outset as any other.

Some ways you can demonstrate respect:

◆ Thank them at the beginning and at the end.
◆ Dress appropriately. If you're wearing a costume, there should be a reason for it and your clothing should otherwise be appropriate to the setting.
◆ Don't make fun of them unless you already have an established relationship with them.
◆ Don't use accents unless you can do them flawlessly and accurately. Imagine an Irish person is in the audience and you use a not-very-good Irish accent. That could be interpreted as mocking them.
◆ Respect your own art and energy. Be on time. Stick to your time limits unless you have permission to exceed them.

- Remember that the audience has lives beyond your performance and might need to go to the bathroom, take that emergency text from the sitter, or other issues.
- Meet them where they are. Treat four-year-olds like four-year-olds and adults like adults.
- Respect that they each come into the performance space with their own baggage, and they are doing the best they can. Sometimes that won't feel like enough.

Welcome your listeners as they are, respect their time and attention, and you will build a relationship with them that encourages repeat bookings, good word-of-mouth and more telling time.

R

Risk

A coaching client once commented that storytelling is dancing on the edge. This man is inventive and courageous in his life and purpose, so I found it interesting that storytelling puts him on the edge of terror and creation that can drive us to new and interesting work.

As I thought about this further, I realized that the edge is part of what I love most about storytelling. From the creative process to the performance, from analysis to the stories I tell, from the vulnerability I see as essential in my work to the ways I help others develop as storytellers, the edge forces me to dance constantly in the moment.

- My **storytelling creative process** is based largely in imagery and improvisation. I do not write my performance pieces before they are told; they require an audience for the very act of creation. I usually start with an image, play with it on my own, maybe talk it through with a trusted ally (though not always) and then simply tell it to an audience, unsure if it is yet coherent, precisely how long it will be and sometimes not even knowing the entire plot. I am selective about which audiences may hear this early piece (I'm not likely to do this at a festival for example) but having the story be heard is essential to its creation. This process is risky, there is always a chance of failure, but I think my early nurturing by Brother Blue gave me this tolerance for risk.

  I *LOVE* this uncertainty. I love how the audience is a necessary part of the creative process for me. Storytelling requires listeners and I need someone to listen to the story out of me. Their reaction will not only shape every performance, but it also gives the story form and structure from the start.

- I do not memorize **the stories I perform**. I know their shape, structure, and sequence of events, with a few crucial phrases committed to memory, but I want there to be room to dance with the audience. Well beyond initial creation, storytelling requires being attuned to the listeners and their reactions. It is a constant dance of creation and destruction, choosing in the moment what to expand upon and what to leave out. When I perform, I am an avatar of Shiva, dancing out creation and destruction over and over again.

- As part of my artistic practice, I revisit my performances and stories regularly, **analyzing and honing the work**. This, too, is a dance on the edge because it requires me to question everything I do. It can easily spiral into great self-doubt and paralysis but it may also lead to insight and deeper work. If I don't take the risk of analysis, I may never improve upon existing work.

◆ When I began performance storytelling, I was in love with telling risky stories, those that pushed me and my audiences to an edge. I reveled in discomfort. I still do, though I am more thoughtful in **the choices I make about the stories I develop and tell**. My earlier determination to go where others did not reflected who I was then. I am now far more comfortable with myself and my art, so I will tell stories that reflect that comfort, but I still delve into discomfort on a regular basis. It makes me stretch as an artist, as a creator and as a performer who cares about her audience. When I tell those stories to appropriate audiences who expect discomfort, it makes my listeners stretch.

It's a dance with discomfort and I continue to learn a great deal about myself and my process.

◆ Regardless of the material I am telling, **I allow myself to be vulnerable** in every performance, consultation and coaching session. While vulnerability is an edge state, it allows a greater connection with my audience and clients. Storytelling is all about that connection, the dance with the listeners because listening is not passive; it's about the moment on the edge when we open up and hold each other in balance.

◆ Lastly, **when I coach, I am dancing on the edge with my client**. Good coaching requires me to be present, to be listening with full attention and to be thinking furiously, all simultaneously. It is a delicate balance between support and constructive feedback. New storytellers or new stories are like toddlers; you want to encourage them, not push them over in your eagerness to help. You want to let the client take advantage of your greater experience as they can, with maybe a few gentle shoves as needed.

Creative endeavors are always risky. They require vulnerability, honesty and a willingness to take the next step forward into the unknown. If we don't risk, we don't grow.

R

A place for your thoughts.

Scary stories

Every storyteller should have a scary story or two in their back pocket

In the context of this book, *scary story* means a story with some kind of supernatural or horrific element (haunted house, movie-style killer) rather than a story of real-life horror (bank foreclosure, natural disaster, real-life murder). These stories give your listeners a delightful chill, not a lingering existential dread.

Whenever I tell stories with kids and ask them what they'd like to hear, they always ask for a scary story. It seems to be what kids are most familiar with in a "storytelling" context, maybe from camp, tv, sleepovers, or from other media sources. Because these stories have such a deep appeal for children, I'd recommend that you have several in your repertoire that are appropriate for younger people. You can always tweak details to make them more appropriate for adults.

The most important element in telling a scary story is you, just as it is in all storytelling. You must care about what you're saying; it's even better if you think the story is creepy. If you are insincere, your listeners will know and won't be drawn into their own imaginations. You can increase the intimacy and believability of scary stories by lowering your voice, lowering the lights, looking around as if you're nervous and telling your listeners you rarely tell this one because it scares *you*.

Some other common elements in effective scary storytelling are:

◆ **Locale.** It helps if you can include regional details your listeners will recognize. It will make the story more believable. This means changing details of the story but not necessarily altering the plot or meaning. As long as you're telling a traditional story or making it up yourself, that's okay. If you're telling someone else's story, then you have already gotten permission and discussed the alteration with them. If you are in a place you don't know, so can't make the story local, then make it local to you. It happened in *your* neighborhood, near *your* school or at *your* summer camp. If it's a traditional story where the locale must remain distant, set that context appropriately. "This is a story from ancient Japan. People still tell it around campfires and they know it's real."

Urban legends are fun to turn into local stories.

◆ **Eye-witness accounts.** If appropriate, for example when telling an urban legend, tell them you heard the story from the person it happened to. This increases believability. If it's something that happened to you, tell them.

- **Vocal control.** If you're telling a jump-tale (a story that ends with a bang so your audience jumps), don't broadcast it ahead of time. Keep your voice at the same volume right up to the yelling part.

- **Select the right story for your audience.** Remember who *you* are and who *they* are. This goes back to basic storytelling technique. If you can't do an accent well, don't do it. If you're a white, middle-aged man don't pretend to be a young black woman if you're telling about a haunted place in the 'hood. You can always say you heard the story from your friend's daughter. Additionally, select the right level of creepiness for your audience. Kindergartners don't need to know all the horrible details, while college students might revel in them.

- **Internal logic.** Be aware of logical holes in the story, especially when telling with kids. If everyone dies in the story then how did you hear it? Kids are good at catching these kinds of mistakes, so be prepared.

- **Practice.** You will be a better storyteller if you practice your craft and approach it as work worth investing yourself in.

- **Suspense.** Everyone may know that the ghost will eventually appear but the question is, when? You can play with your audience as you build suspense by hinting around what might happen, by building in good long pauses, and by letting them know you're in on the joke.

Where can you find some good scary stories to tell that are in the public domain? Folklore is rife with scary stories. Americanfolklore.net is a good resource as is the urban legend database. Remember to tweak those details to make it local. When I tell the vanishing hitch-hiker I always change it to include local details. I bet wherever you are you can find something spooky nearby.

Folklorist Alvin Schwartz has collected many American folktales in *Scary Stories to Tell in the Dark Boxed Set*. Another good book is *The Ghost & I: Scary Stories for Participatory Telling*; I especially like this one because it includes both telling tips and stories for adults and kids. Additionally, the authors have given permission for storytellers to tell these tales.

Have fun telling these tales. Scary stories are among the most dramatic and playful stories you can tell. I'm sure you'll enjoy experimenting with them.

Self-care

It happens over and over again. I let myself get run down and I get sick or I have a head-ache or I'm just cranky. My head is congested, my eyes are watery and all I want to do is huddle in a lump, feeling sorry for myself.

Sometimes I forget that being a working artist is hard work, and I let self-care lag. You might do this sometimes, too. Here are my top five self-care priorities, the things I try to do regardless of how busy things are:

♦ **I try to get enough sleep.** If I can't get a full night's sleep, I at least try to schedule a nap here and there. If I make it my habit to sleep enough then my mood is better, my body can more readily fight off infection and I am more creative/spontaneous/generous in my responses.

♦ **I try to get outside most days.** Even now, when I have a cold, I will at least stand on the porch for a few minutes and breathe fresh air. It helps me remember there is a whole world out there. It also means I take a little time for myself every day.

♦ **I try to do something kind for someone else.** Even at my most miserable, if I can say something nice, give someone a smile or express gratitude, I remind myself that the world is bigger than I am. This shift in perspective can be enough to help me feel better.

♦ **I try to be realistic in my objectives and be kind to myself.** These are related. For example, days when I feel as though I can't think well or focus for long are not the days to write a deep and meaningful story. I'd rather admit that and do the best I can with who I am in the moment. When I can't, when I know I must exceed my current capabilities (say I had a big gig) then I suck it up and do what I need to shine. I then give myself permission to crash later and prepare for that crash ahead of time, since I won't be able to do much at the moment.

♦ **I try to do the best I can, whatever that may be.** Whether self-employed or work-ing for someone else, the best we can is all we can do. I don't get paid if I don't work so I try to avoid sick days (I try to make every day a productive day) but I know it's necessary sometimes. Tomorrow will be something else. If I approach every day as a new *best I can* then each day offers new opportunities. This is self-care because I understand that the *best I can* will change.

Everyone has different self-care needs, but it's crucial to remember that you cannot care well for others unless you care for yourself first. You and your art are worth the time.

Sensory detail

The difference between a good story and great one is often in the details, specifically sensory detail. When you include just enough sensory detail the audience can imagine it that much more thoroughly, their brains will be more engaged, and the story will be more alive for them.

Sensory detail is far more than what something looked like. A brief allusion of a sense can be enough, you need not go into lush detail unless you want to and it's appropriate. Using sensory detail can be a shortcut to the emotional content of the moment. By describing what a moment is like through the senses, you can often convey an emotion with greater impact than just saying someone is sad or happy.

Sight is the sense we most easily reference in stories. This makes sense because our visual cortex is big and we rely on sight all of the time. What the woods looks like, the color of someone's hair, the shimmer of the light on water, these are all easy sensory details to include. Use a little simile now and then to deepen the experience for your audience. "His hair was the color of oak bark" is more evocative than "his hair was dark brown."

Smell is the shortcut to memory. By evoking an aroma in your story, you can quickly set an emotional tone. A room that smells of cinnamon toast and old books will have a different feeling than one that smells of charred wood and rain-soaked paper. Your listeners will all have their own specific associations with the aroma, but by invoking just a little bit of smell, you can quickly catapult them into the story moment.

Sound can be a tricky sense to work in. You don't want to use sound effects or accents unless you're very good at them, but you can describe a sound and its implied emotional response. A voice like velvet differs greatly from one like broken glass.

Taste brings your audience into a whole new sensory realm. The stew may taste good, it may taste like all the meals he ever missed, it may taste like it's hiding something. It could be bitter or sweet, soft in the mouth or chewy as if it had been overcooked and ignored.

Touch is another way to bring your listeners into that exact moment. Be careful with this one, as it can be deeply triggering for some people or may take you in more adult directions than you expected, but it's useful. What if you described Cinderella's experience of feeling the smooth satin of her dress when she was used to burlap? What if you talked about the soft skin of your grandmother's hand?

Kinesthetic senses are a little more complex but can also act as shortcuts. A character might experience something that makes them feel queasy, or they may have butterflies in their stomach. Instead of saying, "she was shocked," what if she had to gulp down the surprise in her throat?

Sensory detail is a doorway for your audience to experience your story more deeply. It conveys emotion, experience, and the moment quickly and effectively.

S

Service

It's hard to define what we do, those of us who make our living as storytellers. It's easy to think of our work as an art, a mystical moment, a craft accessible to all, something obtainable only after years of practice, on and on and on. If we're not careful we can push ourselves to rarified and undeserved heights. When I need to burst my own bubble and come back to earth, I remind myself that I provide a service.

I make my living as a storyteller. I perform, teach, coach, train, and consult, all under the umbrella of the word *storytelling*. I provide services to my clients and I do my best to make sure those services are nothing less than exemplary.

Let's dig a little into what service is and why it's a handy way to think about this kind of work.

First, it is a service. I offer intangible products to my clients, be they an audience, someone working on their own story, a business or non-profit that wants to use storytelling more effectively or a group of people I am training. While I might want to think of myself only as an artist, what I am paid for are services.

Businessdictionary.com defines services as *Intangible products such as accounting, banking, cleaning, consultancy, education, insurance, expertise, medical treatment, or transportation. Sometimes services are difficult to identify because they are closely associated with a good or product; such as the combination of a diagnosis with the administration of a medicine. No transfer of possession or ownership takes place when services are sold, and they (1) cannot be stored or transported, (2) are instantly perishable, and (3) come into existence at the time they are bought and consumed.*

That seems like a good description of performance storytelling. My stories do not transfer possession when I tell them. While they can be stored should I record them, the expertise, craft, and talent cannot be handed over by some kind of mind-meld. In a performance setting, stories are instantly perishable – they exist in *that* moment between the teller and a particular audience – and they come into existence as they are purchased and consumed. This definition stretches to cover coaching, consulting, and training. They are intangible, perishable and momentary. The effects may (and I hope do) linger long after I've gone, but the experience itself is fleeting.

It may be uncomfortable to think of our work this way, as a service. It might feel too businessy, clinical or materialistic, but I find it makes me work harder and serve better if

I remember that my clients deserve the best and, because it *is* a fleeting service, I have an obligation to work as hard as I can for them in my preparation and in the moment so the aftereffects will linger. They are paying for an enduring memory or lesson learned as much as anything.

I also strive to think of my work as this kind of service, as defined by dictionary.com: *service (noun) an act of helpful activity; help; aid: to do someone a service.*

Looking at it this way, I remember that I can never know the full impact of the work. I don't know who I have helped, I know only that I may have been of service. I have been fortunate enough to have people tell me that my work – whether it's a performed story, coaching, or consulting – has had lingering effects, that I helped them. Knowing this *can* happen helps me work harder and strive to be better in the moment.

Lastly, sometimes an experience reminds me that storytelling can be another kind of service: *a form followed in worship or in a religious ceremony or a meeting for worship.*

At its very best, storytelling can play the role of communal service. A group of people gather together in search of a common feeling and create something momentary and sacred. My best moments as a performer, listener, coach, and consultant all have elements of the sacred about them because they connect me to my audience and to something beyond. Collectively we create a moment not soon forgotten.

When I remember that I provide a service, it doesn't lessen the power of what I do. I don't minimize my artistic effort, craft, and talent. I don't feel as though I commoditize or diminish my work. I remind myself that I am on this planet to be of service. I am fortunate that the service I provide is one that serves me, too. Knowing that helps me work harder, dig deeper, offer more and serve better.

It is a privilege to serve the world, my audiences, my readers, and you. Thank you.

S

Setlists, programs, or what stories are you going to tell at the next gig?

Most years in December I am fortunate enough to be hired to tell "Christmas stories" and most years I have a moment or two of panic, thinking *I don't know any Christmas stories!* I do, of course, but I need to review and consider which stories I love, which I find trite, and which will work for a given audience. It is an ongoing exercise in creating an appropriate set list.

For example, when I am hired to tell Christmas stories for adults, I develop a set list based on:

◆ Stories appropriate for adults.
◆ Stories that honor the spirit of Christmas, even though I'm not Christian.
◆ Stories that won't make them uncomfortable, so I think about what I know of the audience.
◆ Stories that will evoke their past and honor their present.
◆ Stories they might not know.
◆ Stories I enjoy telling.

I go through a similar process for most gigs. I realize this may seem time-consuming, but it is important. I certainly have programs that rarely change from performance to performance (Christmas story gigs, for example, are generally pulled from a set list that varies only slightly) but I want to make sure I am honoring this *particular* audience and doing my best to give them what they need based on who I understand them to be, every single time. Reviewing set lists also gives me a chance to find holes in my repertoire and add to it. I can build a set list with flexibility, so it may change when I get in front of the audience, but I find it useful to start with a solid idea of what I will tell, in what sequence, and why.

Building a program can be its own form of storytelling. I make sure the stories I tell feed well into each other and create an emotional arc that may be separate from the emotional arc of each, individual story. You need to decide how hard your audiences must work as they move from one story to the next. Do you want to have a story with a tragic ending followed by something that will make them laugh? Or do you want that tragic ending to be the last word? Each choice creates a very different kind of program.

I also keep track of my setlists in the same program I use to track gigs, so I know I won't duplicate a set if I'm invited back by the same group. This is part of why I consider what stories to tell before every gig; I want to give them something new.

134

Settings

Where does your story happen? The setting is as much a presence in the story as your characters. You needn't over-describe it, but giving your audience a sense of where the story happens is a shortcut to moving the plot along.

The setting creates expectations. The summer of 1968 in New York City differs greatly from Once Upon A Time, though a similar story could happen in each. By placing the action and characters in the setting, you create a world where the story is possible.

Some settings are useful so you can subvert them. Once Upon A Time creates expectations of fairy tales, but if you use that to start a story about your youth, you create that hazy sheen of idyllic memory, which you can then manipulate as you choose.

The level of detail you use in your setting depends entirely on your style, the audience, and the needs of the story. What matters is that it is in a place and time, so you and your audience can explore it together.

S

Sex, the erotic, and the sensual

Sexual behavior and eroticism are a basic part of what it is to be human; the species itself relies upon it. Since storytellers are depicting human experience. It's no surprise that sexual situations may arise (ahem) in your stories, but how you handle them may vary depending on your own comfort, your audience, and the story itself.

Let's start by understanding sexual, erotic and sensual as they apply to storytelling.

Sexual narrative language is about sexuality. It need not be connected with intimacy or affection and has a degree of explicitness. It may or may not be sexy.
> "They got married and got right to work."
> "He didn't know her name but he knew he wanted her."
> "She could feel the heat between her legs."

Erotic narrative language may or may not be directly sexual, but it is about arousal and desire. It may imply eroticism or it may be more explicit, but the intent is to be sexy.
> "Making a baby was more than making love."
> "He watched the sweat run down her neck and imagined he could taste the salt."
> "Her skin flushed and she could feel the heat pour down her body."

Sensual narrative language may or may not be directly erotic, but it is about arousing the senses. It can be appropriate for a wide range of audiences.
> "He felt his heart pounding as he whirled through the dances, the air thick with sweat and hunger."
> "The smooth sweetness of the mango filled her mouth and she closed her eyes."

S

As with cursing in stories, sexual content can be entirely appropriate or way out of bounds. You get to decide if and when you include it, knowing there may be consequences. Here are some things to consider when working with sexual material in told stories.

- ◆ **Why are you including sexual content?** As with any story, you must know why you are telling it the way you are. Does the sexual content add anything to the narrative? Does it make the characters more real, does it add to the moment, are you doing it for effect? Once you know why it's there, you can decide how you want to shape it.
- ◆ **Is it sexual, erotic, or sensual?** Are you describing sexual acts, are you trying to arouse your audience, do you want to pull in rich sensory detail? Your intent will make a big difference in the language you use, the pacing, and so on, so make sure you have a sense of it.

◆ **How explicit do you want to be? What can your audience cope with?** Knowing your own comfort level with sexual material will make this much easier. Knowing what your audience might tolerate helps too. Over-sharing or over-describing can feel self-indulgent and masturbatory if it isn't appropriate to the story.

◆ **If you're going to do it, do it well.** You must be comfortable with this kind of story-telling so the audience will be comfortable. Practice ahead of time.

◆ **Trigger warnings, rape culture and caring for the audience.** Don't forget, many people have had traumatic sexual experiences. Don't spring explicit material on them without some kind of warning. You don't have to interrupt your story to warn everyone that there's about to be a sex scene, but they should know beforehand that sexual matters are part of the performance.

S

Sexism, racism, gender bias, privilege, and other uncomfortable issues

I wish I could say I am without bias, but I'm not. None of us are. It's so easy for our own inherent bias to sneak into the stories we tell without even noticing and with good intentions all along.

Many storytellers would deny their bias, but I have seen and heard examples of sexism, racism, gender bias, heteronormative bias, and others, repeatedly. For instance:

◆ In the U.S. (and I expect in much of the Northern hemisphere Western world) if a character is not described, they are assumed to be white. Most storytellers describe the color of someone's skin ONLY if they are not white. What's more, many fairy tales described the loveliest as the "fairest" and the wicked as "dark."
◆ I've heard dozens of male storytellers use a high squeaky voice for female characters. I don't talk like that and I bet most women they know don't either.
◆ Unless the storyteller is LGBTQIA, the relationships in the stories are almost always heterosexual between cis characters.

I could go on and on, but you get the idea. I'm not saying that white, straight characters are a bad thing, but that representation matters. Strive to be aware of your own bias as a storyteller and gently work against it. You never know who is in your audience and will appreciate that the most beautiful girl has brown skin, or that the male hero loves to bake, or that the princess falls in love with another princess.

Privilege is another uncomfortable issue at play in the life of the performing storyteller. We are privileged to do this work. Not everyone can engage in what they love, whether as a hobby or as a vocation. It's important to remember that each of us is functioning from a position of some privilege, whether that we were lucky enough to experience storytelling and have the a-ha moment from listening; that we can take the financial risk of being a working artist; that we have community support of some kind; or some other experience of privilege. I am not suggesting storytellers give up our craft and work in the salt mines, but that we recognize how very fortunate we are.

Because storytelling is a transformational art and one that moves people so deeply, we can use it to build empathy and fight social ills, but first, we must recognize our own biases and privilege, and be willing to use storytelling to expose inequity. When we listen openly and tell with authenticity, we can change the world.

Sourcing

I love traditional material. I hold a degree in folklore and mythology and have never stopped exploring the world of traditional stories. I tell many folktales and myths, but I am careful about what traditional materials I cover. I want to be sure that I am not stealing someone else's work, so I check my sources.

If a work is published after 1900, you must confirm it's in the public domain. You can do this by contacting the publisher, though it's often a more complex process. A quick internet search will usually help you find more information. Newmediarights.org has a nice chart that may help and copyright.com has some other useful search resources.

Many storytelling organizations ask their tellers to have **three separate sources** for the traditional stories they tell. For example, I may find a version of Snow White in one of Andrew Lang's books, in a collection by Jane Yolen, and in a picture book at the library. Each version has subtle differences in plot and phrasing. I can cite these three examples as proof that the story in its most basic form is in the public domain.

My personal version of the story must be distinct from all three cited examples. Storytellers do not get to steal the intellectual property of other artists. If we tell a version of a story that isn't our own creation, we must have permission to do so or it must be a piece wholly in the public domain. I may tell Snow White word for word from Andrew Lang because it is in the public domain. To be ethical, I should cite my source and make sure my audience knows this version isn't original to me but was written by Mr. and Mrs. Lang. I may *not* tell Jane Yolen's version without her express consent. How would you feel if someone told one of your stories verbatim without your permission?

Once I have my sources, I then **play with the material**. I love doing this. I think about the story from different points of view, I imagine the settings, I engage my senses, about what most resonates with me in the tale. I create my own version of the story. We all can do this. We may be inspired by Jane Yolen's telling, but we can all take the same plot elements and put our own interpretation onto it. Start with senses and what you love. Get someone to listen to you. Dream aloud.

S

If the story you want to tell is literary – it was written by someone and is original to them AND it is not in the public domain – then you must get their permission to tell it. It's good ethics to cite them when you tell the story and not claim it as your own.

I have made mistakes but generally, these guidelines work for me and for my students. I know the stories I perform are mine to tell. I know I am not stealing anyone else's work, that it is my own intellectual property. It's not a lot of work, when you get down to it, to make sure you aren't stealing.

S

Speaking out loud: Diction, comprehensible speech, pacing, rhythm, the "storyteller voice," and pauses

As storytellers, our voice is our instrument. We could be telling the best, most meaningful story in the world and it wouldn't matter if our audiences don't understand us.

- **Diction.** Your speech must be clear and your words should be well enunciated to the best of your ability. Speak so your audience can understand you. You needn't sound like a BBC radio announcer, but make sure you aren't mumbling.
- **Volume.** Public speaking can be scary and you may speak quietly if you're nervous. Hold your head up, take a good breath, and remember that your audience wants to hear you.

  Sometimes, it is hard to know if you're loud enough, for instance when you don't have a microphone. In that case, I have asked my audiences to raise a hand if they can't hear me, so I know I must speak up.
- **Speed of speech.** Many storytellers, myself included, speak too quickly. When we do, it's hard for people to understand you and there isn't time for them to absorb what you're saying before you're onto the next sentence. Take your time.

  An ideal rate of speech is somewhere between 120–160 words per minute; many audiobooks are around 140 words per minute. It's more pleasant to listen to people when they vary the speed of their speech. You can use speed to indicate mood and action, so experiment with it.
- **Ums, ahs, and likes.** These interrupted speech patterns are very common but don't have much of a place in performance storytelling. Practice your stories, record yourself and listen for the verbal interruptions, then practice again. As you practice with an eye to minimizing verbal interruption, they will fall away from your stories. Don't beat yourself up if it happens occasionally, just be aware of it next time.

  We also use interrupted speech patterns to avoid silence and pauses. A moment of quiet can add great emphasis and drama to your telling, so don't be afraid to be quiet for a beat.
- **Rhythm.** The cadence of your speech will help your audience know what's going on. For instance, if a character is engaged in dull work, you could use the rhythm of your speech to indicate the repetitive and tedious nature of the task.

S

◆ **Storyteller's voice.** Some storytellers have a telling voice that's notably different from their everyday speaking voice. It's often much more of a sing-song cadence or highly theatrical. I would encourage you to stay away from storyteller voice and instead learn to make your everyday voice more musical. It will help you remain authentic to yourself.

◆ **Pauses.** A well-timed pause in a story serves many purposes. It helps your audience catch up with you. It can indicate a moment of suspense or drama. It can be quite comedic with the right facial expressions. It gives you a chance to gather your thoughts if you've gotten lost. I'm not suggesting extensive William Shatner-like pauses after. Every. Word. An occasional pause will help you slow down, help your audience catch up, and will help your story be understandable.

S

Stage fright

So often when I tell people I'm a performing storyteller they respond with, "I could never do that! I'm terrified of talking in front of people!" Stage fright is a very common phobia and one that must be managed if you want to perform in front of others. Here are some questions I am often asked about stage fright.

◆ **Do you have stage fright?** Of course. It doesn't happen with the same ferocity that it did when I first began performing, but it still happens. Fear of public speaking is one of the most common phobias, so it's easy to be overwhelmed by it. By this point in my career, I rarely have significant stage fright, but I remember what it was like and I feel great sympathy for anyone who suffers from it.

◆ **How do you deal with it?** The first thing I do is remind myself that no one out there wants to hurt me. They are on my side. Storytelling is a forgiving art.

I try not to focus on the fear but on the relationship with the audience. I remember to love them.

I remind myself that if I make a mistake, I know how to deal with it.

I remind myself that this is my passion, my life's work and that it is a gift only I can give to this audience at this moment.

I remind myself that I have done this before.

I remind myself that the things I am feeling that I associate with fear (rapid heartbeat, tight breaths, tight stomach, sweating, etc.) are all also associated with excitement. Maybe I'm just excited about the story I'm going to tell.

Once I've reminded myself of these things, I close my eyes and take some slow, deep breaths. As the oxygen floods my body, my heart rate slows. The sweat cools. My throat and stomach loosen. The oxygen suffusing my cells tells every part of me there is no reason for fear. I am safe.

◆ **What if that doesn't work? What if you make a mistake or forget something?**
Then I make a mistake. It's unlikely the audience will storm the stage and tear me limb-from-limb. It's more likely they didn't notice. If I can and if it's necessary, I just weave the mistake back into the story. I say something like, "Now what you didn't know, what I didn't know and what the hero certainly didn't know is...." It sounds like elegant craftsmanship. If the audience noticed the mistake or if it's a mistake I need to own up to (like forgetting a big part of the story and it's something I can't just weave in) then I smile and say something like, "The funny thing about storytelling is that sometimes storytellers make mistakes. I forgot to tell you that..."

Then I take another deep breath and keep going.

S

◆ **How can I get over stage fright?**

Practice your material in front of a loving audience.

Remember to breathe. Ask yourself regularly if you're breathing. All that oxygen helps immensely.

Remember your audience is on your side.

Afterward, ask someone you trust to tell you what went well. Don't ask for criticism, just praise. As you gain more confidence, feelings of stage fright become less important.

S

Story elements in oral storytelling

Every told story comprises five elements:

1. Character and point of view
2. Setting
3. Voice
4. Plot and conflict
5. Context

Additionally, stories have a structure and can be told in linear or non-linear ways, you can read more about that in the structure entry.

Character and point of view

Every story has characters. There are the expected characters – the protagonist, the antagonist, secondary characters, the love interest and so on. There are also unexpected characters, such as very minor characters and elements of the setting (more on that below). Expanding your idea of character gives you more elements to play with.

Let's look at a common story, say Cinderella, and see who's there.
Protagonist: That's pretty obvious, Cinderella
Antagonist: Again, no question, the stepmother and sisters
Love interest: Who else? The prince
Minor characters: In most tellings, the only obvious minor characters are the fairy god-mother and sometimes the father
Unexpected characters: This is where it gets fun. Disney does a nice job with this; in Cinderella minor characters include the mice. The pumpkin coach even has its own personality.

S

Setting

The setting itself is an important element in the story. Imagine if, instead of the woods, Red Riding Hood walks through a sunny field or down an urban street. It changes the story. Taking some time to describe the setting also gives you a chance to get the audience's imagination working and lets them drift deeper into the telling.

Voice

Most traditional tales are told in the third person, most personal stories in first. Third person allows you to be an omniscient narrator, sometimes with a wink to the audience, while first can be much more intimate.

Plot and conflict

These are the basic elements of your story. What happens, to whom and what are the results. This helps differentiate a story and a mild anecdote. A story has a specific sequence of events that result in something being different at the end. An anecdote may not.

Context

Who are you telling to? What will make sense to them? What do they need to hear? Understanding your context when you tell stories means you can make better choices about what to tell and how to tell it, you can be appropriate to your audience, the physical environment, weather, current events and more.

Structure

Every story has a structure. A simple structure could be: start at the beginning, tell the middle and go to the end. A slightly more complex structure might start at the end then tell the events leading up to it.

S

Story Triangle

Every storytelling experience is about managing a set of relationships between the teller, the story and the audience. The story triangle is a dynamic interaction among these three elements present during any storytelling experience. The teller, story, and audience interact so the story experience is different every time. The story triangle itself is derived from Aristotle's rhetorical triangle, which encompasses reason, character, and emotion.

Rather than emphasizing narrative elements, the story triangle focuses on the players and relationships present during a storytelling event. This happens within a context, the setting that influences each individual element and the relations between them. Make sure you consider the setting, the light and noise levels, the other extenuating circumstances (for instance news events) when you facilitate relationships between teller, tale and audience.

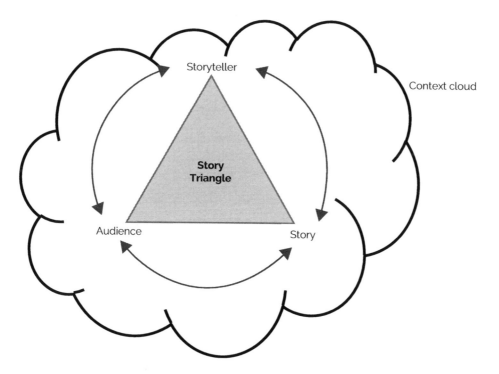

The Storyteller

The simplest definition of *storyteller* is one who interprets, shapes, and expresses the story. Whether they're telling their own material, a traditional story, giving a speech or presentation, the storyteller's choice of words, tone and body language makes that story uniquely theirs.

The Audience

The audience takes in the story as told by the teller, and uses the teller's words and performance cues to interpret the story. They draw equally on their own life experiences though that is often not a conscious process. They react to the whole story and its individual parts by applauding, laughing, crying, yawning, etc. Their mere presence affects the storyteller and the story. While a story may exist before it is told by the storyteller, even in written form, the primary and most important place a story exists is in the individual minds of the audience during the story experience.

The Story

The story itself has a life apart from both the teller and the audience. Stories are both containers and triggers. As containers, they carry and convey characters, experiences, events, and even worlds to a listening audience. As triggers, they set off sparks and flashes of recognition and meaning within the minds of the audience. Like a chemical reaction, stories can bond to the life events of the audience, allowing stories to feel more authentic. By identifying with the characters and events of a story, we sometimes can see our own lives differently. We see what the characters see, we learn what the characters learn. Stories fulfill both container and trigger roles simultaneously. They can present the new and the old, the novel and the recognizable to an audience.

The Context

The context is the setting within which the storytelling experience happens. You may be able to control quite a bit of it (for instance if you're giving a house concert) or you may not be able to control much at all (you're at an outdoor festival or large-scale events are happening in the world). Our job, as storytellers, is to acknowledge the context, allow for it where we can and give the audience a way to become immersed in the story despite the context. This might mean changing the story, choosing a different story, asking everyone to come in closer or other ways of helping your audience connect to you and your story.

Beyond the main story triangle participants as individuals, we now can consider the relationships that happen within the context of the world and the other events around a told story.

The storyteller and the story have a relationship.

The teller studies, thinks, practices, builds their story. They consider their movement, language and more. The story is shaped by the teller. It is an intimate relationship.

The storyteller and the audience have a relationship.

The audience watches and listens to the teller, absorbing their interpretation of the story. The teller, in turn, watches the audience and responds to them. Because storytelling is such a fluid art with little or no fourth wall, the teller can change the story as needed to meet the needs of the audience. Does the audience really love trees? Fine, spend more time in the forest. Does the audience not appreciate your humor? Fine, let's move on.

But *the most important relationship* in the storytelling performance experience is the relationship between the audience and the story.

As tellers, we can't control this. All we can do is craft our story and pay attention to the audience as best we can. It's what happens in the mind and imagination of our listeners that makes the magic. *Every single listener* will interpret your words and actions in their own way, colored by their own experiences. *Every single listener* will hear a different story. *Every single listener* will have their own relationship with the story. Yes, the teller is the vehicle that allows it, but our job, as tellers, is to do the best we can, then get out of the way and let our listeners' infinitely creative minds dance with the words, the images, the narrative.

I am awed every time this happens. And it happens every time I trust myself, my story and my audience.

S

Structures and motifs

Story structure is the way the story is told and developed; what happens when to who, and how. When developing your story, you can set audience expectations by using a familiar story structure and then playing with it. When you use a recognizable story structure, the structure does some of the work for you by helping the audience know what may be coming next; you just have to fill in the narrative detail.

Standard story structure begins with an introduction to the characters, setting, and plot. It introduces some kind of complication that the protagonist must overcome, then adds more complexity to it. The climax of the story allows the character to solve the principle problem. The denouement continues the resolution and the coda, if there is one, is a glimpse into the events beyond the ending, or a moral is revealed.

We can also think of structure as a formula that makes building a story easier. Satisfying stories must have beginnings (A), middles (B) and endings (C). It can sometimes be hard to figure out each part, so if we think of the story structure as a formula, that may make it easier.

Some common formulas are:

A-B-C
> Once there was this person/event/thing. These things happened. It ended this way.

A-B-A
> Now-then-now-conclusion/how things change
> Here-there-here-conclusion
> My story-your story-my story

C-A-B-C
> Begin with the end, then tell the events leading to it. A story that starts with a flashback might use a structure similar to this one.

Most stories also contain familiar motifs. A motif is a recurring fragment or theme in a creative work, such as a recurrent melody or a familiar idea. The wicked stepmother is a motif, as is searching for a lost shoe.

Any small theme that recurs in many stories can be a motif. Audiences like motifs because they don't need explanation; they already have a cultural context built in. Someone is stealing lunch – this is an annoying problem. Everyone is working towards an IPO – they are working hard, long hours and are probably very excited. The cultural context is assumed.

Stith Thompson, a folklorist who worked out of the University of Indiana, developed the seminal Motif-Index of Folk-Literature that lists and describes thousands of motifs and tale-types (classifications of different kinds of folktales). If you explore this six-volume work you may find some you can weave into your own stories.

When you tell your story, you can help the audience along by using a familiar motif. For example, if you're telling a love story and a character loses a shoe, your audience may jump to the idea of a Cinderella story. You can fulfill that expectation or subvert it, but it's still a quick way to suggest action. Motifs are familiar to your audience, so it's a shortcut to moving the story along.

There are all kinds of ways you can play with motif and structure. All give you a chance to both propel the narrative with shortcuts and to play with audience expectations.

S

A place for your thoughts.

Technology vs. storytelling

Humans are storytelling creatures. I start just about every class I teach with the comment that storytelling is arguably our oldest art form, that our brains literally evolved for storytelling.

We tell stories every day, even if we also use technology to communicate every day. Whenever we interact face-to-face with another human being, we are likely to tell a story. On a routine basis, people say to me that storytelling is a dying art. I strenuously disagree; we still tell stories. We still *need* stories. Even if other media appear dominant, storytelling is as basic a part of being human as upright walking is. We're not going to stop telling stories any time soon.

There are numerous fMRI studies that demonstrate how active the brain is during sto-ry*telling* as opposed to other methods of conveying information. The gist is that when we tell and listen to stories, our brains are deeply engaged. In fact, the brain of the teller and the listener mirror one another; there is even some anticipatory effect in the listener's brain, so they are looking ahead in the story. Oral storytelling is as close to telepathy and precognition as anything we've scientifically observed. Because our brains are innately primed for *heard* story, storytelling evokes empathy and emotional resonance more immediately than any other way of conveying information. This means we connect more to stories than to text messages, written language or videos. This alone reassures me that storytelling is not going anywhere.

It's easy to be distracted by technology. When writing my computer, connected to the internet, I want to stop writing to check Facebook or my email. I feel the pull, yet I know my writing has meaning, so I keep going. So it is with performing arts; we help our audiences fight the pull of technology and distraction for just a little while.

Performing artists have a responsibility to our audiences to help them remember their basic storytelling and listening selves, and there is meaning in a story. When we ask them to set aside their technology for a few minutes to pay attention to the story, we give them a chance to reconnect to this ancient and powerful part of their brains.

I expect it has been a struggle to communicate across generations for as long as people have been communicating. I'm certain way back in history there were a bunch of people complaining about papyrus, that it would distract young people from learning the old ways. I'm certain the told stories of the ancient Egyptians differed from their written counterparts, just as the written versions of my stories differ from the spoken. But one

T

supports the other. We can use these new technologies to gain an audience, to share ideas, and to deepen our understanding of the art. We as performing artists must adapt and change with our times as we keep this ancient art alive. The two can co-exist if we are willing to do the work.

It is normal and natural for new technologies to seem disruptive. Because storytelling is wired into our brains, it will not be replaced by any technology any time soon. It is our responsibility as performers (and therefore as teachers; audiences must be taught how to listen, remember?) to help our audiences connect to themselves. I'm sure everyone reading this has experienced the storytelling trance when listeners are enraptured. Give audiences a chance to get there. Invite them to take the time and listen. Invite them to transcend distraction and, for just a little while, find themselves enraptured.

T

Tenderness

It's easy to focus on the negative connotations of tenderness such as "easily hurt," "weak or delicate," "immature," yet the word has other meanings that have relevance to performance storytelling and art-making in general. Not tough. Gentle. Moved to emotion.

We all enter the world as tender beings. We are vulnerable, soft, delicate, moved to emotion easily. As we grow, we toughen up, hiding the tenderness that still exists under the skin because it is too risky, too vulnerable to let it show.

New stories are tender things, like babies or those new shoots poking out of the ground, requiring a gentle touch to grow into the rugged and powerful moments on stage. When we recognize the tenderness at the beginning, we are less likely to be frustrated when the story grows at its own pace – you can't hasten a flower by pulling on the stem. When we remember the tenderness of the beginning, we can approach each telling with joy in the creation, with wonder that it even exists. When we let glimmers of our own tenderness show – say the affection we hold for the villain, the truth that a story still has meaning to us – the audience may be more likely to let themselves experience it all more deeply.

How do you allow tenderness into your art? Here are some possibilities.

◆ In early development, let yourself feel how a story affects you. Ask yourself why you are drawn to it, why you feel how you feel about it. Understand your own tenderness.
◆ Appreciate the tender moments in the story. What happens when the protagonist sees their love for the first time? What about when we remember the shame linked to a part of a personal narrative? If we let ourselves feel those things as the story develops, we can more easily communicate it to our listeners.
◆ Let yourself feel tenderness for your characters and narratives. Sure, your bad guys may be reprehensible, but if you understand where they are tender, they will be that much more believable and maybe just a little bit sympathetic. When your audience can sympathize with the villain, they fall more deeply into the story and are left with more to think about. Even Disney villains have a tender spot we can feel for – Scar (the villain in The Lion King) has been overlooked for his brother his whole life. The wicked queen has only her beauty for comfort and is deeply betrayed by the mirror's honesty.
◆ Honor your own tenderness throughout the process. Don't think you need to become hard and cynical to become an effective teller. Leave room for your own heart and the hearts of your audience. Some of the best, funniest storytellers I've ever heard have tenderness at the core of their narrative.

T

Therapy, emotions while telling, and over-sharing

Without a doubt, storytelling is a therapeutic art form because it connects listeners and tellers, reminding us that we are not alone and our experiences are not isolated. It can be used in a therapeutic setting, but it's important for the performing storyteller to remember that the audience is not their therapist.

Our job, as storytellers, is to share stories with such skill and craft that the audience can have their own experience of the story without having to worry about taking care of the storyteller. This means if we tell a story we find personally difficult, we must perform it so the audience doesn't know we still find it hard. This doesn't mean we shouldn't be vulnerable; vulnerability helps connect us to our audience. What it means is that we shouldn't lose control of ourselves while on stage. We must have done enough of the emotional work before the performance that we can tell the story and remain safe.

There are some who believe we can only tell stories we have thoroughly processed. Others believe storytelling is inevitably a kind of therapy so it's okay to tell truly raw pieces and fall apart on stage. Both of these are extremes: If we wait to tell a given story until we have thoroughly processed the emotions attached, we may never tell certain important stories, but if we use storytelling performance as a substitute for therapy, we violate the trust of the audience by forcing them to worry about the teller and sabotaging their own experience of the story.

I have seen storytellers become emotional on stage and handle it with aplomb. They take a minute, acknowledge what is happening, and then move on. The audience feels privileged to have witnessed something so authentic, but they don't feel as though they need to stop their own emotional process to heal the storyteller. It was still a successful performance.

I've seen storytellers fall apart on stage, to a point where the audience feels as though they must help the storyteller and no longer feels safe experiencing their own emotions. These were not successful performances because the storyteller's need outweighed that of the audience.

I've also seen storytellers who have done the emotional work and can tell the story without falling apart, but they overshare to a point where the audience isn't comfortable.

Their own need for self-revelation is more important than what makes a good story. Those were also not successful performances.

- **I try to head the problem off by practicing.** If I know a story is likely to evoke a response I don't want to reveal in my performance, I can make it predictable and so build a pause into the performance. There is a point in a particular Crazy Jane story where, every single time, my throat gets tight. Since I know it's coming, I now have a natural pause there, so I have a moment to swallow before I continue. Practicing also helps me develop some insulation from the emotion, so I am less likely to have an unexpected response than if I'd not practiced.
- **If I do have a strong, unexpected response, I can often counter it by imagining the next part of the story as PowerPoint slides.** Nothing sucks the emotion out of a moment more than PowerPoint. If I can pause for a beat, see the bullet points of the next scene as a slide, I can usually regain control over my wandering emotions pretty quickly and easily. You may need a different metaphor from PowerPoint, this works for me.
- Lastly, if I need a moment, if I get teary or need to take a breath, **I remind myself that storytelling audiences are generally very understanding.** I may pause, take a breath, smile and thank them, then continue. I find audiences appreciate honesty and vulnerability enough that, as long as I don't run off the stage sobbing, they understand and will give me a little latitude. I should add, I have never needed to stop entirely. I've always practiced enough that I was able to continue with a deep breath or two. Professionalism matters.

Equally, when we work with others, we must have done our own emotional homework. When we run workshops or coach people, we must be able to guide them through emotional experiences without being their therapist. Remember that story is important, but it is not a substitute for a therapist when one is needed. We also must be able to set boundaries so everyone in the workshop has equal time and no one person becomes an emotional black hole.

When working on stories that bring emotions to the forefront, work on them enough that you can be reasonably sure that you will not hijack the audience's attention. When you help others with their stories, guide them to therapeutic help if it's beyond your ability to manage. You can be vulnerable, honest, authentic, AND honor the audience's experience of the story.

Timekeeping, timing, and accordion stories

Most of your gigs will probably come with time constraints. You are asked to tell a five-minute story at a slam or to deliver a 55-minute keynote. It's important to have a solid understanding of how long your stories are, so you can put together good sets. Storytellers who don't memorize their stories may find this more challenging, but with practice, you will know about how long each story is. It is your responsibility and a reflection of your professionalism to make sure your stories fit the allotted time. When you go too long, you are giving the message that your work matters more than that of the other tellers or the organizer's plan. When you're too short you may appear unprepared. Neither of these may be true, but there is an underlying message.

I keep track of how long each story tends to runs. While I don't memorize them, by the time I take a piece onto the road beyond my neighborhood open-mic, I know about how long it will take. Knowing this allows me to build effective sets and to respect both the organizer and any other performers. If I am familiar with the organizer, I might ask them for a five-minute warning, so I know when I should wrap up. Sometimes I put a clock on the floor of the stage or wear a watch. I make sure I understand how long I have and what I want to say.

Not everyone is mindful of time like that. At some point in your storytelling work, you will probably find yourself with more or less time on the stage than you expected. Maybe the person on before you went a little too long or maybe someone else didn't show up; either way, you must change your set.

It helps if you have a couple of accordion stories under your belt. An accordion story is one that can be easily modified on the fly to be longer or shorter. It may sound daunting at first, but it's not that hard to develop and even easier to use, with just a little practice.

What makes a good accordion story? First, you need to know the story well. You should have a solid, consistent version of it you can tell on the fly and without difficulty. Second, it must have a simple plot at its heart; it also must have room for extra characters and scenes if you need to expand it. Third, you need to like it. Accordion stories require on-stage flexibility, so it helps if it's something you enjoy telling and want to play with.

For example, you might tell Red Riding Hood as an accordion story. A short version, about five minutes, is the simplest, with Red heading into the woods, ignoring her mother's warning, meeting the wolf, going to grandma's and getting eaten. A longer version, up to maybe 10 minutes, might incorporate more imagery and emotional context. A third version, longer still, might add in additional characters like the woodsman or more about the mother. It might include something about why the wolf is so hungry. You could play with this in many ways to make it a longer and still interesting story.

T

Truth

Truth is such a tricky topic. One person's truth is another's lie. Witness reports always vary. How do we handle truth in storytelling? I get asked this a lot when I'm helping someone work on a personal story. How much truth is too much? What if a detail or two is changed to make a better story or to protect the innocent?

If you're considering telling a true story and are concerned about how true it needs to be or if the truth might be damaging, ask yourself the following. The answers will help you understand how you should craft the work.

If the story is your story, it happened to you:
You own the story and the events in it. You get to tell them because they are your truth.

◆ Will telling the truth hurt/embarrass/damage you or anyone else? If it will, are you willing to accept the consequences? If you're telling the story to enact revenge on someone, I'd suggest letting this one rest for a bit longer.
◆ If you choose to change it (and frankly that is usually my advice if the story will be damaging) how can you change it without altering the things you most love about it, the truth it conveys?
◆ What happens if you just change names, locale, dates, etc.? Is that enough? If you don't want to change those things, ask yourself why.
◆ Is it appropriate for your audience as it is? If not, why are you telling them this story in particular?

If this is someone else's story and they gave you permission to tell it:
You know the person it happened to, they said it was okay to tell.

◆ Have you talked with them about the parts you might want to change? What did they say?
◆ You *are* planning to tell the audience this happened to a friend and not to you, right?
◆ If you change it, does it alter the truth of it?
◆ Is it appropriate for your audience as it is? If not, why are you telling them this story in particular?

This isn't your story and you don't have permission to tell it:

◆ If it isn't in the public domain and you don't have permission, then stop. It isn't yours.
◆ There are literally millions of stories in the world. Can you find one that you don't have to steal?

T

Uncomfortable

It's easy to do what's comfortable. For instance, I love telling fairy tales. I love telling twisty, difficult, dark fairy tales. Some people find this surprising; they think it must be hard to tell these stories because they go in such odd places but for me, it's not. It's comfortable, I enjoy the imagination and metaphor.

What has been uncomfortable for me is telling personal stories. For years, I avoided it, telling any kind of fiction, myth, and folktale instead. I told people I had no personal experiences to tell stories about. It was so uncomfortable, I turned down gigs instead of revealing things about my life in any factual way. Eventually, a kind friend helped me to craft stories from my life. Light ones at first and then increasingly difficult stories. It wasn't easy and it wasn't comfortable but spending time with that discomfort and working through the problems telling these stories presented made me a much better storyteller. I now can tell personal stories with ease, but it took time and a willingness to live in the discomfort.

When we go to the places that discomfort us, we grow. It's the same thing when we use our bodies; we need to be a little strain to build new muscle and endurance. Try using storytelling in new ways. Try telling the kinds of stories that you find challenging. Try telling to audiences you might have avoided. Tell from an uncomfortable perspective. Find safe ways to do so and you will grow. What was a struggle might become your new favorite thing. At a minimum, you will stretch in new ways, learn new skills, and know your limitations are farther away than you thought.

U

Unexpected audiences

Despite the best-laid plans, sometimes you walk into a gig and find you have an entirely different audience than the one you expected. It doesn't happen often, but when it does, you need to deal with it.

I start by trying to avoid this situation altogether. When I am hired, I ask a lot of questions prior to the event, including who is the expected audience? Have they run this event before and, if so, who showed up? How is it being marketed (which tells me something about who may come)? Will someone be introducing me and, if so, could they please mention muting phones, etc.? I couch all of this as being in the service of giving them the best performance I can. It's really in the best interest of the person hiring me to make sure I know what to expect. I don't make this about me and my need, but about setting appropriate expectations for all parties involved.

Most importantly, I find out who will be the accountable person onsite. When I arrive at the scheduled time (always well before the performance), I introduce myself and remind them about phones, no recording without permission and whatever my preferences are regarding photography. I smile. I say *please* and *thank you*. I am as gracious as I can be, so if there is a problem and I ask for help solving it, I don't appear to be petty.

I think about set design in three ways; this is covered in greater detail in the setlists entry.

◆ If I know there is a reasonable chance my audience will change, I try to design my set lists with some flexibility though I remain focused on the announced intent of the show. For instance, if I'm hired to tell stories in 6th-grade classrooms and get bumped into the 4th grade, most of the material is likely to still work with a tweak or two.

◆ If I am hired to tell stories to adults at a show advertised as 18+ but some parents bring little kids, I ask the organizer to remind the parent about the advertised content. I may check in with the parent. Then I tell essentially the stories I was planning on. The parent made an informed choice. I might tone it down a little but not by much; maybe this parent routinely brings their kids to R rated films.

◆ Lastly, if it is an event with a specific set that cannot be changed (i.e., Crazy Jane, Woman on the Edge, or another one-woman show) I go ahead with it exactly as planned. These events typically occur in more controlled settings like theaters, where the audience expectation should have been clearly set. I may ask the organizer to remind the audience this is an evening of stories for adults.

If the audience is radically different from what I was expecting and it isn't an immutable show, I do my best to adapt but I make sure I talk with the organizer, so they know this isn't okay next time. I have a number of standby-sets appropriate for certain audiences, tried and true stories that work with younger people or mixed groups. I'll use one of those if I must. There are also many, many stories appropriate for all ages and I make sure I keep some of those in my rotation at all times. For example, many folktales operate on the Sesame Street principle – amusing for younger people with lots of jokes they won't get but bigger people will.

As far as interruptions and other unexpected events, I play with them. If a phone rings more than once, I may step out of the story to ask them to mute it or I may incorporate the sound. If a child is screaming and won't be quiet, I may ask a parent to step out for a moment so the other listeners aren't disturbed. Again, having a good relationship with your organizer helps; they may intervene for you. In general, I try to remember that life is always happening and we need to be compassionate as performers. Sometimes that means ignoring it, sometimes it means gently incorporating or acknowledging it.

Ultimately, that's what storytelling is: dancing with the audience, dancing with the moment, and trusting the story to carry us.

U

Unknown

You've prepared for your gig. You've learned your stories, organized your set, researched your audience, had a light and sound check, you're ready to go. There will always be factors you can't control. Maybe you're telling at an outside venue and the weather changes. Maybe a little kid wanders up on the stage. Maybe a significant global event changes the nature of the world, making some of your stories less than ideal. You don't know what will happen. All you can do is adapt the best you can. Throw in a story about how the rain is really the stars weeping. Incorporate a brave little kid into your story, then invite her parents to scoop her up. Acknowledge that the world is a difficult place and we need stories to help us through the dark.

The unknown is present in every performance. While some of it might be difficult (the weather, the kid, the world), you can also revel in the unknown. It might lead you to create a new and wonderful part of your tale. The story triangle means we collaborate with the unknown worlds inside of our listeners.

Solving for X, working our way through the unknown, lets us be more creative and grounded in the present instance. It encourages us to be flexible, to dance with the story, our audience and the very moment.

Consider the trains that frequently run through the National Storytelling Festival held annually in Jonesborough, Tennessee. It's a wonderful event with some amazing stories. The town itself is a lovely historical place with a freight line running through the back. Anyone who tells at Jonesborough risks having a lengthy freight train become an overwhelming accompaniment to their story. It is a very large and loud X.

I've seen tellers break out of their story and into new tales about trains. Others whistle or tap in time with the rails. Still others simply wait, smiling. Those who try to overwhelm the train with their voice, continuing their story, are the tellers who get lost and risk losing their audiences. By embracing X, the train, flexible storytellers can build a greater relationship with their audience. By overcoming the adversity of the freight train's roar, they gain the sympathy of the audience and they can, sometimes, inject a note of play and fun by dancing with the inevitable.

U

Venues

There are as many venue possibilities as there are stories. Some are expected (festival stages, open mics, slams) and some are not. I've told stories in some odd places, including on an airplane.

I was waiting for a delayed flight and got to chatting with the pilot waiting for the same plane. When I told him I'm a storyteller, he was fascinated and asked all the questions I have come to expect. What do you do? Who are your audiences? How did you get into it? And then his face lit up.

"Would you like to tell a story on the plane?"

I froze. And then said, "Yes!"

Half an hour later we boarded. After apologizing for the delay, the captain told everyone there was a professional storyteller on board and, if no one objected, she would tell a short story. Once the passengers gave their consent, we took off.

I must tell you, I was anxious. I've been telling stories for decades and rarely get that nervous anymore but telling to a captive audience was nerve-wracking.

Halfway through the flight, I went to the front of the plane, was told how to use the intercom, the captain gave me a lovely introduction and I began. I told a simple version of *There's Always Room for One More*. It seemed appropriate for an audience sitting cheek-to-jowl on an airplane. As I told, I could see people all the way down the airplane leaning into the aisle to see. I think, mostly, they liked it. They applauded politely and smiled as I walked back to my seat. I honestly can't tell you if they enjoyed it or not, but I know it made for a nice distraction while traveling.

I'm telling you this story to help you remember that venues are everywhere. If you have a broad repertoire, you'll be able to pick a story appropriate for the place and the audience, taking advantage of every opportunity. Have fun and remember that being a storyteller, sharing your tales, is a gift for the weary traveler and enraptured audience alike.

V

Violence

For better or for worse, violence has a place in some of the stories we tell. Many traditional fairy tales are terribly violent, We tend to censor out the worst part but think about how awful it is that the wolf is cut open in Red Riding Hood. It's a very violent moment in an equally violent story. How you handle violent parts of your stories makes all the difference between a traumatized audience and a powerful moment in a story.

As with other challenging moments, know why you need the violent scene. If it's just for shock value, ask yourself how important that is to you. Why do you need to shock everyone? If the audience is shocked, they won't pay attention to the rest of the story. If the violence plays a purpose and has a reason to be in the narrative, then you must decide how detailed you will be and how long the violent scenes will take.

For example, you can simply say "The woodsman killed the wolf, helped granny out, and they all lived happily ever after." That's not too bad and would be appropriate for younger or more sensitive audiences. If you were telling this story as an environmental analogy, you might have reason to detail the wolf's pain. That would be appropriate for a different audience. You must know why you are using violence in your story and how you want it to be received.

Sexual and assaultive violence require more consideration. If a rape or domestic violence scene is part of the story, make sure it is essential to the tale. Think about how explicit you need to be and ask yourself why. You don't know who will be in your audience, and retraumatizing them (or yourself) is unkind.

Once you know why the violence is there and how you will handle it, make sure your audience is prepared for it. If appropriate, put a trigger a warning at the start of the program.

There is a place for violence in stories, just as there is a place for sexuality, humor, grief, and all of the other human experiences. Because of its traumatic nature, violence deserves special consideration. Remember, storytelling has tremendous neurological power and abusing the empathy and immediacy it creates is not how to build a storytelling career or a way to serve yourself or your audience.

V

Voice and vocal care

Our voice is our instrument. We must learn how to control our voices in many ways to be effective speakers. As you prepare for your performances, ask yourself:

◆ **Can my audience hear me?**
Have appropriate amplification for your venue. Your needs will be different in a theater, a gym, outside and in an office. An audience composed of elders will have different needs than preschoolers.

◆ **Do I know how to use the amplification equipment?**
Make sure you have time for a sound check and understand how to modulate your volume when you have an amplifier.

◆ **Do I know how to protect my voice?**
If you don't have amplification equipment, know how to project, how to protect and how to most effectively use your voice. You can learn more about this from a voice teacher and other storytellers.

Some things to be wary of include whispering and vocal fry (making your voice sounds gravelly). Both can damage your vocal cords if you're not careful.

◆ **Remember to breathe, remain hydrated and hold yourself upright.**
Because our voices are our instruments and are part of our bodies, we must treat our bodies well. Take deep breaths. Drink some water. Stand up. You'll feel better and sound great.

◆ **If you encounter vocal or lung problems, don't mess around with them.** See a doctor. If you were a carpenter whose hands weren't working well, you'd get help. As a storyteller, your voice is as important as the carpenter's hands.

◆ **Consider taking voice lessons.** Learn how to control your breathing more effectively, expand your range, and use your voice without hurting it.

The voice is really nothing short of miraculous. When you tell a story, your brain wraps images and ideas in language. That language is made audible by contractions of your vocal cords, movements your tongue, lips and teeth, and air expelled from your lungs. Those vibrations in the air then move through the world, until they reach the tympanic membrane of your listener's ear, where they are interpreted and turned into the listener's own images and ideas as shown in the story triangle. The voice allows a direct route from one mind to another. Relish it. Respect it. It will carry you to new and unexpected places.

V

Vulnerability

Performance storytelling, at its best, is about connection. It's about creating a piece where the teller can say *here is something I know to be true* and the audience can sigh back in recognition of their own truth. Whether it's a fairy tale, a personal story, a historical yarn, or something else entirely, when storytellers are at our best, we are bearers of truth even if it's through metaphor. When we connect with the audience and share that truth, we together become something greater than a narrative, a voice, listeners.

How does this happen? In my experience, it's a combination of skill, practice, passion, talent, authenticity, and vulnerability.

In Brene Brown's fantastic TED talk on vulnerability, she builds a case for connection giving meaning and purpose to our lives. She says that when we embrace vulnerability when we allow the imperfect self and yet still are compassionate with ourselves, we become more connected to one another and are more alive. It's the storyteller's job to build connection. That is the heart of our art. We allow ourselves to be vulnerable and to connect with our audience, we change the world.

When I stand on stage and tell you stories about Eve loving her flawed husband, about the city of Ys drowning in the waves, about Jack loving the Giantess, about Crazy Jane embracing her madness, about love and fear, about my own struggles with depression, about my husband's death, about the things I did as a little girl, I am vulnerable. The story may be funny or poignant but I am revealing myself to you, my audience. I embrace that. It is the revelatory moment allows us to connect.

When I tell, when I'm in the vulnerable state, if there is a particularly visceral image, I let it wash over us both. Each and every one of you. I trust you to go there with me, so sometimes I might close my eyes for a moment. I perform barefoot, so I can feel the world beneath me, but this leaves me vulnerable to physical harm. It's worth the risk to open the door for connection.

V

You, too, become vulnerable when you are in the audience. You are being asked to open up enough to let the story mean something to you, so as you laugh or sigh or gasp, I am breathing in your vulnerability and using it as a tool to be more open in turn.

This is part of what made my mentor Brother Blue such a transformational storyteller: when he was in the room there was no one wilder or more vulnerable, so that meant it was safe for everyone to experience their own wildness and vulnerability. When I tell and reveal myself, it becomes safe for you to do so, too.

I'm not suggesting storytellers use the stage as personal therapy. Letting ourselves be open and vulnerable when we perform is the opposite of therapy. It's what happens when we know who we are, understand and still love our own flaws, and accept what our story means enough that we can offer it whole-heartedly. It is a model to the audience of what it means to live with enough bravery to be vulnerable.

Once I have worked through the parts of a story that scare me the most and I understand its meaning I can be vulnerable and remain safe as I perform. I can give my audience permission to feel whatever they need to, to be as vulnerable as they wish as they sit in the dark and listen.

Together we create connection. Together, we can be imperfect and still whole. Together, during the story, the world holds its breath and sighs with us.

A place for your thoughts.

Who, what, where, when, why and how

Do you remember, in maybe fifth-grade writing class, when your teacher told you that all essays needed to answer six crucial questions? Storytelling is no different. The six crucial questions, five Ws plus one H, give you and your listeners the basic information required by most stories. Remember, simply answering these questions will not make the story a great one, but it will give you a foundation to build on.

◆ **Who.** Who is your story about? What are their characteristics? If the story is about a girl, make it about a specific girl. Make it about the girl who sat three rows ahead of you in class, the one who always wore the same ribbon in her hair, the ribbon that got dingier over the year, the one who didn't come back to class after the class queen bee stole it from her. Make your *who* specific. We want to know what happened to that girl with the ribbon. If it was only about a girl, we wouldn't really care. What's more, you can use one *who* to lead to another. I never knew what happened to her but I always wished I had stepped in.

◆ **What.** What happens matters. Decide what the girl cares about. She cares about the ribbon. The ribbon is stolen. What happens next? *What* is the action that moves your narrative forward.

◆ **Where.** Stories need to live in a place. The more carefully you paint the place, the more easily your listeners can go there. Use all your senses, not just vision. What is carved into the wooden desktop? What does the classroom smell like? What does the light look like just before the ribbon is stolen? If this story is from your life, or if you want it to have a real-world setting, give that to us. *Where* is more than physical space, it's setting and mood.

◆ **When.** This encompasses not only literal time, but emotional and personal time. When I was in third grade. When the world was young. Between the wars. Each *when* places you and your listeners in a time and provides context. Oh, this is a creation story. Oh, this is a personal story. Oh, this is a...

◆ **Why.** The motivation, the drive, the cause for the action. This can be tricky, because you may want to leave some of this shrouded in mystery or even entirely unexplained, but you must provide enough explanation that the audience can connect to the actions in the story. The wolf is wicked and hungry. The queen bee is acting upon her nature, preying upon the weak. The girl with the ribbon... well, that might be a place to leave enough white space for the imagination to run wild. The speaker who didn't intervene was afraid, becoming the character we all know in our secret hearts. The *why* gives the listeners something to latch onto and identify with.

◆ **How.** *How* brings everything together. How did the who commit the what? What's more, *how* allows you to paint a clearer picture – how did the girl's face change when she saw the ribbon dangling from the queen bee's fingers? How did you feel when you just watched?

Using these basic questions will help your stories be deeper and more interesting for your audience. They will help you show rather than tell details about your world. They will give you an opportunity to decide where you want to insert white space and where you want detail, reminding you that what you say and how you say it matters.

One story two ways.

Version one.
When I was young, I remember there was a girl in my class who clearly didn't have much money. Her name was Frannie. She wore the same clothing most of the time and always had the same ribbon in her hair. One day Justine, the class bully, stole the ribbon from her when the teacher was out of the class. Frannie cried and screamed until she could barely breathe. I think she was sent to the nurse's office by the hall monitor who ran in, while Justine pranced around with the ribbon. I just stood there and watched. The teacher took the ribbon and put in her desk. But we didn't see Frannie again. I wonder what happened to her.

Version two.
I was a pretty shy kid, especially in middle school. I remember my fifth-grade class seemed like it was full of yelling and spitballs. I pretty much kept to myself and drew with my scented magic markers, they were all the rage then. A few rows in front of me was Frannie. I was grateful to her because she was the reason I could be invisible. She was poor. Her clothing smelled because she didn't wash it often enough. She always wore her hair the same way, tied back with a greasy red ribbon and, in fifth grade when fashion was starting to count, this was her biggest sin. She would rub its soft sheen against her cheek, staining it darker each day.

One afternoon the teacher told us all to be quiet while she went to talk to the principal. Most of were. Most, except for Justine and her clique of Bonnie Bell lip gloss wearing friends. They surrounded Frannie and commented on her clothing as if she weren't there. "Did you see what that smelly girl had on the other day?" I remember thinking someone should do something, make them stop, but I wasn't that someone. I guess everyone thought that. Frannie did nothing, just sank down into her chair a little more.

W

Then Justine snatched the ribbon from Frannie's hair. "Look, I have a snot rag from her hair!" She held it between two fingers, high above Frannie's head. Frannie screamed then, a high wail. I'd never heard grief like that before. I don't think I've heard it since. Justine and her girls laughed while Frannie screamed louder, her face the color the ribbon might once have been. A grown-up came rushing in. Justine ran back to her seat, holding the ribbon in the air like a flag the whole time. Frannie kept screaming. The adult tried to calm her down, but her scream didn't stop. I didn't know how she could breathe.

Eventually, the room was full of adults. Someone picked Frannie up and carried her, like a portable siren, out of the room. Someone said something about a nurse. Our teacher silently took the ribbon from Justine and put it into her desk drawer. She locked the drawer, and tried to teach us the capitals of Europe, though no one was paying attention. Justine couldn't stop giggling.

Frannie didn't come back to our classroom, not that afternoon or that week or that school year. I wondered why none of us said anything. I wondered where she was. I wondered what happened to her ribbon. Did it stay in the desk drawer all that time, hiding so no one could see it? Did the teacher cover it with papers so she wouldn't remember? Did it go someplace where stains don't matter and it's only the soft satin that counts?

Why

Why do I tell stories? Why do I get up on stage in front of people and talk? What do I love about storytelling?

I do it because I can't not do it. I can't not do it because it is a basic part of being human – we are the storytelling animal – and because it is a basic part of my truth in the world. Story matters. My voice matters as does yours. This is not a manifesto but maybe it's the beginning of one. It is incomplete, but it is what I know in this moment, which is all we ever have anyway.

I love the connection. The visceral rush, the near-telepathy that comes with connecting to an audience. I love our combined breath, the gasps, and sighs that come as I move through the narrative. It is as though we become one animal, constructed of story solely to turn words into a living moment.

I love the mystery. There are times when I tell stories that it feels as though the universe is speaking through me. I listen to the story coming out of me as much as I construct it. I love the sense that I am part of something so much bigger. It's similar to the feeling I get when I look at enormous natural beauty, that awe for the world and my minute-but-integral place in it.

I love the variability. Every time I tell a story it's different. It may be something I've told a thousand times, but because the audience is different. because we are at different places in our lives, the story is different. It is new every time and yet ancient, in my bones.

I love the dance between teller, tale and listener. The story triangle is a description of relationships, but it also describes motion. We are all dancing together.

I love the listening required to tell a good story. I must listen to my audience, to myself, to the world to be a better storyteller and teacher.

I love the solitary work that goes into the performance. Spending time with books, words and my own thoughts gives me a chance to consider what's important to me. What I want to share. What matters enough in this world that I will make myself so vulnerable as to step on stage and say, "Here I am."

I love the timelessness of it. Stories endure. I can tell a tale 3000 years old and it is still relevant. I can tell another I made up yesterday and it connects. What's more, storytelling removes me from the present moment; I go into a kind of trance when I perform or listen deeply that frees me from my cares and worries. I am transcended.

I love the connection with the past. The old tales link me to generations of dreamers, of tellers, of listeners. Through them, I can see into my own past, the past of my ancestors, the dreams of those who have gone before.

I love the connection with the future. Every time I tell stories, the audience might go away changed. They may tell stories themselves. Words loved and shared have power.

I love the accessibility of storytelling. **Everyone** has stories to tell and **everyone** should be heard. I love helping people find their voice, bloom as they realize that their story matters.

I love telling stories because of the places it takes me, the people I meet, the thrill of standing on stage, the one-on-one connection, the risk and success and failure, because of the change it creates, the ways it makes the world bigger, the notes I receive saying "now I know I am not alone." I love telling stories because of how it challenges me, because I am transformed, because it is sometimes an ecstatic thing, because of the glow I see on your faces. I tell stories because it is a way of earning my living that brings value to the world. And there is occasionally beer.

I love telling stories because it helps me craft the world with you.

Story matters. My voice matters as does yours.

Do you know your why? Think about it. The answer might change your world.

Wow

Ultimately, *wow* is what we should be saying after most of our storytelling experiences. Not all, sure. There are always the crummy gigs, the ones where the kids just didn't want to listen, where the parents talked over you, where you forgot something crucial, where your slides didn't work, where you just weren't into it, where it didn't gel. It happens. But most of the time we should come out of our storytelling work saying, *yes, this. Wow, that was fun. I did something meaningful.*

Why devote our lives to something that takes so much work and time if we will not enjoy it? If we will not feel as though we made a difference in the world?

We are so lucky to be storytellers, whether it's what we do for full-time employment, as a hobby, or if we incorporate storytelling into our other work. We are so lucky to know this art form is a basic part of what it is to be human, to think and talk and live in story. We are so lucky.

My friend and mentor, Brother Blue, used to say that the room was full of angels, regardless of how many visible people were there. He was right. When we tell stories, we evoke our own best selves, we become beings of voice and image and breath. We remind ourselves of what we could be. We remember the connection one human can make with another. We are saying *I'm here. I'm alive. I have experienced this, dreamed this and am sharing it with you. Now you can experience it, dream it.* If that's not a wow I don't know what is.

W

Xenophobia

Xenophobia:
An unreasonable fear or hatred of foreigners or strangers or of that which is foreign or strange.

Storyteller and writer Annette Simmons has wisely said that *Storytelling is an antidote to war*. My friend and mentor, Brother Blue, believed that storytelling was the path to world peace because *How could you kill someone if you know their story?*

Storytelling strips the mask away from xenophobia. When we hear stories from people we consider foreign or strange we can recognize our shared humanity or we can embrace mindless fear and hatred. We can't do both. We must choose and we are revealed. It is in the stories, that we find ourselves and our common ground. By listening we dare to set aside fear.

Shared stories break down boundaries. When we listen to folktales or myths from another culture, we recognize our own. When we listen to someone tell stories about their life, their family, their hopes and dreams, we recognize ourselves. The U.S. military understands that we can change more hearts and minds through storytelling than we can with bombs. They have funded multiple studies that show repeatedly how stories – told and heard – create empathy and change. More than guns. More than handouts. Stories give us a no man's land where we can find ourselves reflected in another's eyes. If the military gets it, maybe we can, too.

Brother Blue's statement may seem over the top, but isn't it worth trying to connect with those we may find frightening before we lash out? Isn't it worth telling them a tale or two and listening to their stories first? What's the worst that happens if we try to set aside xenophobia and find common ground? War and prejudice can always be a second option. In this world, where it's so easy to make assumptions, where we're told we should be on the attack, taking the time to listen becomes a radical act.

Maybe storytelling *can* save the world. It's at least worth a shot.

X

A place for your thoughts.

Yes

There are so many pressures on us all the time, it's easy to just say no to things that seem like they might be too much work or too tough. There are times when storytellers should say no, but that being said, I think it's very important to say yes to the world, yes to the things that scare you. When I want to grow and stretch, I do something that frightens me. It need not be a big thing, but something that moves me out of my comfort zone.

My mentor, Brother Blue, was a believer in saying yes. He said yes to all kinds of things and had amazing adventures. He said yes to work, to people, to life in a way that very few others have. I try to emulate him with mixed success.

In my professional life, I sometimes say yes to things I will be good at but might not yet have material for. I say yes to adventures. I say yes to things I know will make me stretch and learn, so I will then know if that experience is one I want to repeat. I don't say yes to the paid gigs I already know I am not good at, instead I refer that work to those who can represent storytelling more effectively, but I may experiment with similar material in environments where I won't damage my reputation or that of storytelling in general.

This applies to most aspects of my life, well beyond storytelling. While there are some things I'm pretty sure I will not like (very crowded places, for example) I generally try to be open to possibility.

Storytelling is about opening ourselves, our audience and our world to possibility. It is about saying yes to the possibility we are creatures of wonder and hope. It is about saying yes to the possibility of connection with strangers, to the gift from the old woman in the road, to the possibility we may be able to heal.

When we say yes to storytelling, we say yes to connection, to the next adventure, to the road that may lead to happily ever after, whatever that may mean to you.

Take five minutes and embrace the world. Yes.

Y

Yes, and...

Yes, and... is the first rule in improvisational comedy. It's also the first rule in the life of a storyteller.

Every experience is fodder for the next story. You see a hippy walking a toy poodle? Great, that could be a story. Your mother calls and talks your ear off? That's story fodder too. You accept life experiences, joyful or tragic, participant or observer, as opportunities for stories, even if you may never tell the obvious story in front of you. Maybe that toy poodle is really a magical servant. Maybe it's a hallucination personified. Maybe the hippie is really a breeder of rare dogs. Maybe it was inherited from their just-deceased stock-broker son. You don't know the story, so you can make it up. It's your story now. Even if you don't use the idea immediately, add it to your compost heap, a file that contains various ideas, phrases, and inspirations for stories.

Yes, and... also means that you're willing to risk failing. If you work on a story that doesn't go where you expected or you get stuck, it doesn't mean it failed. It means you learned something new about your own process and maybe you should move on to a different story. This one will wait for you.

Frankly, *yes, and...* is a nice rule to have for life in general. I try to go through the world saying *yes, and...* I encourage you to try it, too. Regardless of how you're using it, *yes, and...* will help. Working on a speech for your Rotary club? When someone asks a question try *yes, and...* Stuck in a story? Try having someone say something outrageous about a character and respond with *yes, and...* You get the idea, right? "Yes, and..."

Y

Zeal

Storytelling is what you make of it. So is life. As storytellers, we get to choose what content we present and how we present it. We get to choose whom we present it to and how much we want to connect with them. So it is with life. While we may not be able to choose our circumstances, the stories within which we live, we have considerable choice about how we respond and whom we share it with.

What seems to matter, in the end, is this: Be kind to yourself, to your audiences, to those with whom you walk through the world. Be aware of your needs and the needs of those around you. Make your choices and then do the best you can with the results, because that's all any of us can do.

Diligent enthusiasm helps. When we do the best we can with all the enthusiasm we can muster, life and work feel less like chores and more like opportunities to do something new, create change, reach for new heights.

Z is for zeal. Tell with intent. Love your audience. Live big. The world is waiting for your stories and for you.

A place for your thoughts.

Some thank yous

This book would not be possible without the love and support of Kevin Brooks, Charley Shaffner, my parents Florence and Harvey Packer, the Brooks children, Christie Keegan, Amy Langlois, Mary Stewart, Serene Josiah, Mark Binder, Ruth Hill, Brother Blue, Marni Gillard, Scott Moore, Danielle Bellone, Rachel Ann Harding, Kevin Kulp, Marie-Helene Grzesiak, Loren Niemi, the porcupines, StorySpace, and many others. If you are feeling hurt that your name isn't listed, it's only because I am fortunate to be so well supported that I didn't list everyone and I needed to finish the book.

The team at The Small-Tooth-Dog Publishing Group has helped me turn this dream into a reality with support, suggestions, and great teamwork.

I am especially grateful to the readers of my blog. Thank you especially to those of you who commented on my blog, sent me private notes, or commented on other forums. It means the world to me when I hear that something I said was useful or meaningful. If you want to use this material in other forums, please let me know first. Let's talk.

A few people deserve an extra bit of appreciation:

Thanks to my still-beloved Kevin Brooks, who brainstormed many of these ideas with me. I couldn't have done this without him and I miss him every day.

Thanks to my beloved Charley Shaffner, who walks through this life with me and puts up with more sociability than any introvert should have to.

Thanks to my readers (Florence, Charley, Danielle, Ann), editors, family, friends, storytelling colleagues, and more.

Thanks to you, for reading the thank-yous, not to mention the rest of it.

The adventure continues. I think happily ever after really means they had a cup of tea and then got ready for the next adventure. I'm sipping my tea and can see the next adventure around the corner. Ready? Let's go!

35162037R00108

Made in the USA
Middletown, DE
03 February 2019